THE SPIRITUALITY OF TEILHARD DE CHARDIN

SISTER MARIA GRATIA MARTIN, I.H.M.

Sister Martin has focused on the whole of Teilhard's spirituality and shows the interrelation of its various aspects. She provides the reader with a synthetic presentation of Teilhard's views, both scientific and Christological, as the basis of his spirituality. This gives to her book a distinct value among the plethora of Teilhardian writings.

The Spirituality of Teilhard de Chardin is undoubtedly an important book.

THE AUTHOR

SISTER MARIA GRATIA MARTIN, I.H.M. was educated at Marygrove College and received her master's degree from the Catholic University in Washington, D.C. She has taught religion to both elementary and high school students and is presently chairman of the Religion Department at East Catholic High in Detroit.

Sister is an active member of the Chicago Religion Teachers Association; has served on the Detroit Archdiocesan Human Relations Education Committee; and is working on her community's Liturgy Commission.

She is part of an experimental, structureless religious community living in conjunction with the newly formed Sacred Heart Rehabilitation Center for alcoholic men in Detroit.

THE SPIRITUALITY
OF
TEILHARD DE CHARDIN

The Spirituality

of

Teilhard de Chardin

by

SISTER MARIA GRATIA MARTIN, I.H.M.

NEWMAN PRESS

Westminster, Md.   Glen Rock, N. J.   New York, N. Y.

Amsterdam   Toronto   Montreal

ACKNOWLEDGMENTS

Excerpts from books listed below reprinted by permission of Harper & Row, Publishers.

THE FUTURE OF MAN by Pierre Teilhard de Chardin, translated from the French by Norman Denny. Copyright 1959 by Editions du Seuil. Copyright © 1964 in the English translation by William Collins Sons & Co. Ltd., London, and Harper & Row, Publishers, Incorporated, New York.

THE DIVINE MILIEU by Pierre Teilhard de Chardin. Copyright 1957 by Editions du Seuil, Paris. English translation—Copyright © 1960 by Wm. Collins Sons & Co., London, and Harper & Row, Publishers, Incorporated, New York.

THE PHENOMENON OF MAN by Pierre Teilhard de Chardin. Copyright 1955 by Editions du Seuil. Copyright © 1959 in the English translation by Wm. Collins Sons & Co., Ltd., London, and Harper & Row, Publishers, Incorporated, New York.

THE MAKING OF A MIND by Pierre Teilhard de Chardin. Copyright © 1961 by Editions Bernard Grasset. Copyright © 1965 in the English translation by William Collins Sons & Co. Ltd., London, and Harper & Row, Publishers, Incorporated, New York.

HYMN OF THE UNIVERSE by Pierre Teilhard de Chardin. Copyright © 1961 by Editions du Seuil. Copyright © 1965 in the English translation by William Collins Sons & Co. Ltd., London, and Harper & Row, Publishers, Incorporated, New York.

THE APPEARANCE OF MAN by Pierre Teilhard de Chardin. Copyright 1956 by Editions du Seuil. Copyright © 1965 in the English translation by William Collins Sons & Co. Ltd., London, and Harper & Row, Publishers, Incorporated, New York.

Published by Newman Press
Editorial Office: 304 W. 58th St., N.Y., N.Y. 10019
Business Office: Westminster, Maryland 21157

Printed and bound in the United States of America

Contents

Preface

In this age of the "God is dead" theologians and the dynamic new laity, the new liturgy and the new nuns, the new city and the new breed, demonstrations and dialogue, instant participation in battles and U.N. debates via the living room TV, the urgent call of the inner city and the cry of the "atheist" for Christian relevance, experimental religious communities and "experimental marriage," there is understandably enough some unrest among those who have been seeking Christ along the traditional paths of Christian spirituality. Underlying this unrest there seems to be a basic quest for authenticity. Where *is* Christ? How do we *experience* Him? How does He reveal Himself and how do we let Him reveal Himself through us? How do we open to His Spirit, and how, in fact, do we serve Him? Dizzy with their new realization of the sacredness of the secular, some have proposed a new spirituality for the secular city, a spirituality that seeks the *real* Christ in people and in the events of our day, and serves Him in the *real* work of building the secular city, but at the same time rejecting as meaningless the barren "imaginings" of prayer and the "self-centered" ascetical practices of the past. The tremendous insights of our age into the *real presence* of Christ in people and in events should of course be cultivated and lived. But in our own experience and that of many others this is impossible without the intense faith and an uncompromising sincerity that come from deep prayer and a certain conscious self-discipline. In any event, to reject prayer seems to contradict the very personalist foundation of the new insights; for a genuine relationship with Christ would seem to demand at least as much open and intimate presence-response dialogue as that required by deep human relationships. This contemporary version of the prayer-action tension seems to have an unprecedented urgency, flowing as it does from a dawning realization of the Christian's, and in fact mankind's, cosmic dimensions and his responsibility for his world and the progress of his era.

The spirituality which Teilhard de Chardin preached and lived seems to us to indicate with remarkable simplicity and depth the direction that we of the secular city should take in our search for Christ. Flowing as it does from his vision of Christ everywhere giving a face and a heart to the world, it satisfies the contemporary Christian's deepest longings to find Christ *where He is,* both in the people and the world in which He is becoming, and in the intimacy of the heart where He speaks face to face. In the pages that follow we hope our readers will share the joy that was ours in studying Teilhard's thought and searching for the foundations of his spirituality. We have summarized our findings rather concisely in the foreword. Those who are not familiar with Teilhard's thought may find it incomprehensible by its very conciseness; if that is the case, it would be better to skip it and begin with the introduction, and then come back to it at the end.

Foreword

Teilhard de Chardin's spirituality as outlined in *The Divine Milieu* is the logical flowering of his evolution-oriented Christological synthesis. In a universe seen as a converging cosmogenesis directed towards unification in spiritual synthesis, human endeavor is the only means of universal progress. Since the material universe will reach the term of its evolution in the co-reflective vision of a united mankind, human endeavor is ultimately a process of assimilating the universe of matter into collective thought and simultaneously increasing man's personal unanimization in love which alone enables him to attain the highest cosmic synthesis. The ultimate energy of evolution, therefore, is love, the only power capable of uniting human reflective centers. Since all union can be achieved only on a level higher than that of the elements uniting, the union of human persons can only be achieved by their common incorporation into a transcendent union with a pre-existent Person in whom each is centered and fulfilled and opened out to all others. A collective awareness of this personal Center of universal convergence or Omega is the ultimate requirement for the total unanimization of mankind and the personalization of the universe in mankind united. Such an Omega, known and loved, activates the human thrust of evolution not only by thus drawing mankind to union in love, but also by guaranteeing to the human laborer the permanence of his works as part of the cosmic body of an immortal mankind.

Christianity is the only religion that can provide an evolution-conscious mankind with a coherent and satisfying view of the universe. Christianity reveals that Christ Jesus, dead and risen, is the Omega of cosmic evolution and that by His redemptive Incarnation continued through the Eucharist He has transformed

cosmogenesis into Christogenesis, that is, into progressive unification in Himself as His cosmic Body. In the light of Christ's revelation of the Trinity and science's understanding of cosmogenesis, Creation, Incarnation and Redemption are seen as interrelated
and continuous divine acts effecting the unification of created
multiplicity within the interpersonal relations of the Triune God.
This continuous process of creative union draws the universe in
man to Jesus, the Incarnate Word, as His cosmic Body, His created fulfillment or Pleroma, by means of the Eucharist and in a
way that reflects the inner activity of the Trinity. Through the
Eucharist, Christ-Omega in union with the Father and the Spirit
unites to Himself first the intimate communion of believers and
then, through their faith-inspired labors, the whole of mankind
and the material universe.

Christian labor and suffering and prayer are the interrelated
aspects of Christian spirituality as Teilhard presents it in *The
Divine Milieu,* a spirituality which is ultimately a mysticism of co-
creative union with the Trinity through the Eucharistic Christ.
Fidelity to God's will demands that the Christian more than any
other man should labor earnestly to further universal progress for
the love of Christ whose cosmic Body he is co-laboring with the
Father and the Spirit to build. Through his active acceptance of
suffering the Christian, inspired by the Immaculate Virgin Mary,
yields to the purifying action of God operating within him to
achieve his own unification and completion, and thus to make
him a more perfect instrument of cosmic unification. Only an
intense, ultimately mystical, awareness, attained in prayer, of
Christ's universal presence can enable the Christian, in purity and
faith, to assimilate the universe into himself-in-Christ and simultaneously to unite his uniquely and partially redeemed world
with the whole universe assimilated into the Eucharistic communion of believers-in-Christ. Teilhard's spirituality or mysticism,
therefore, is essentially and simply the collaboration, in faith and
adoration, with the Trinity in the progressive realization of Jesus'
priestly prayer that all may be one in the very union of the
Father and the Son by the Spirit.

Having compressed Teilhard's theories as much as we could in this brief synthetic vision of the universe illumined by Christ as he saw it, there remains for us now the task of examining more closely the components of that synthesis, so that in the end our vision of the whole will be richer and more deeply convincing.

Acknowledgments

It is with deep gratitude that I acknowledge the invaluable assistance of Father Robert Faricy, S.J., without whose patience, interest and fine direction this manuscript would probably never have reached its final form. I am also indebted to my parents for the typing as well as their enthusiasm for my work, and to my I.H.M. sisters who read the manuscript and offered much encouragement.

INTRODUCTION

The Key to Teilhard's Synthesis

"Lord, grant that I may see, that I may see *You*, that I may see and feel You *present in all things* and *animating all things*."[1] This simple prayer contains the key to Teilhard's whole spirituality, particularly what we might call his "mysticism of action"; and in some degree it must be the prayer, also, of anyone who wishes to understand his thought. At the very beginning of *The Divine Milieu*, Teilhard invites us to place ourselves at his "privileged position," that is, to look from the vantage point of the fullness of Christian revelation and to see what he sees: the Universal Christ at the heart of the world, penetrating all things with His active and tangible presence and revealing by His presence the meaning of all human experience.[2]

Throughout my life, *through* my life, the world has little by little caught fire in my sight until, aflame all around me, it has become almost completely luminous from within . . . Such has been my experience in contact with the earth—the diaphany of the divine at the heart of the universe on fire . . . Christ; His heart; a fire: capable of penetrating everywhere and gradually spreading everywhere.[3]

It was in the growing light of this "diaphany" that Teilhard developed that "particular point of view . . . of the relationship

[1] P. Teilhard de Chardin, probably a personal note, written at Peking, October 20, 1945, quoted in Henri de Lubac, *Teilhard de Chardin, The Man and His Meaning* (New York: Hawthorn Books, 1965), p. 28.

[2] *The Divine Milieu* (New York: Harper, 1960), p. 15, hereafter cited as DM.

[3] DM, p. 15.

1

between the fulfillment of this world and the kingdom of God" [4] which became the bedrock of his spirituality. In its light he could integrate within himself his love of God and of the world. He could plunge into his research, "into the crucible of the world of tomorrow," [5] with "an absolute integrity and the complete utilization of all his powers," [6] convinced that "God is obtained by carrying through our tasks as men," [7] and even more, that by our labor "we bring to Christ a little fulfillment." [8] "There's a prayer," he wrote to his cousin Marguerite, "that I'm fond of saying now because it sums up what I mean: 'Jesu, sis mihi mundus verus.' May all that is elect in the world, Jesus, be to me a channel for your influence, and be increasingly transformed through my efforts into you." [9] It is interesting to note that perhaps the clearest and most concise summaries of Teilhard's spirituality are to be found in his prayers; evidence, it would seem, of the fact that his inner "totalization," his reconciliation of the traditional action-contemplation tension, came as the fruit less of speculation than of experience, mystical experience.

Nevertheless, although the light may have dawned in prayer, it was preceded by long nights of search and struggle. "The intimate relationship," he writes, "between my Christic and cosmic sense and their definitive co-existence in my heart, produced in the depths of my soul a conflict between the God of the 'Upward' [reached in prayer and by detachment from the world] and a new type god of the 'Forward' [reached in labor and dedication to human progress]" [10]—a conflict, he admits, that

[4] Letter of July 30, 1918, in P. Teilhard de Chardin, *The Making of a Mind* (New York: Harper and Row, 1965), p. 224, hereafter cited as *MM*.

[5] "La Foi qui Opère" in *Ecrits du temps de la guerre* (Paris: Grosset, 1965), pp. 307-29 (hereafter cited as *Ecrits*), in P. Teilhard de Chardin, *Hymn of the Universe* (New York: Harper and Row), p. 95, hereafter cited as *HU*.

[6] "Le Milieu Mystique," *Ecrits*, pp. 137-67, in *HU*, p. 118.

[7] Letter of July 30, 1918, *MM*, p. 224.

[8] *DM*, p. 31.

[9] Letter of July 30, 1918, *MM*, p. 223.

[10] "Le Coeur de la Matière" (unpublished) p. 24, quoted in Christopher Mooney, S.J., *Teilhard de Chardin and the Mystery of Christ* (New York: Harper and Row, 1965), p. 28.

was always the problem of his life.[11] Teilhard's efforts to resolve this conflict in no way represent a compromise between two opposing loves, God and the world; it is rather a perfect illustration of "faith seeking understanding" in order to believe more ardently in the Christ of Colossians in whom "all things were created" and in whom "all things hold together." [12] His thought focused, therefore, on a fundamental vision of the co-extension of Christ with the universe, such that:

1) Christ takes on the grandeur and enveloping power of the universe, and
2) meritorious action can be performed with the consciousness of acting in union with the whole universe.[13]

The synthesis that he worked out on the basis of this vision he longed to share with his contemporaries whose minds,

set upon interior unity, become the victims of a veritable spiritual dualism. On the one hand, a very sure instinct, mingled with their love of being and taste for life, draws them towards the joy of creation and knowledge. On the other hand a higher will to love God above all else makes them afraid of the least division or deflection in their allegiances. In the most spiritual layers of their being they experience a tension between the opposing ebb and flow caused by the attraction of the two rival stars . . . : God and the world.[14]

If the above passage reveals very clearly the conflict of Teilhard's own soul, the following extract from a letter written early in his career gives us an insight into the anguish with which he experienced the dilemma. We quote it at length here because it will serve as a springboard into the development of thought by which he intellectually resolved it.

I mean the problem of reconciling progress and Christian detachment —of reconciling a passionate and legitimate love of all that is greatest in Earth, and the unique quest for the Kingdom of Heaven. How can

[11] Letter of March 15, 1916, in Henri de Lubac, *The Religion of Teilhard de Chardin* (New York: Desclee Company, 1967), p. 243.
[12] Col. 1: 16, 17 (RSV).
[13] "Mon univers," *Oeuvres de Pierre de Chardin,* IX (Paris: Seuil, 1955-65), pp. 272-3. (9 volumes—hereafter cited as *Oeuvres.*)
[14] *DM*, p. 20.

one be more Christian than any man and yet be more man than any? It is an excellent thing to study the sciences or philosophy or sociology, in order to please God, and to carry out a task that has been given to us. But that is not saying enough: so long as, in my studies or my work, I cannot see any possibility of loving my task; so long as I do not see that I must devote myself to it so that, precisely by means of what I win by it (and not only because of the moral value of my efforts) I may advance and bcome an organic being in an Absolute; so long as the World appears to me only as an opportunity to acquire merit, and not some eternal possession to be built up and embellished—so long as such things can be said, I shall be no more than a half-hearted laggard among men, and they will look on me as being (and blame my religion for it) something less than a full man, and a turncoat. And would anyone feel justified in saying that they are completely wrong?

I am concerned, therefore, in order to satisfy myself and to 'systematize' my interior life, to find out what there may well be (of divine in)—what may be predestined beneath the very matter of our cosmos, of our humanity, of our progress. And I feel drawn to the study of the currents, the links, all the things 'in nobis sine nobis' which carry us along, and which we direct into channels, which we instinctively worship and against which we fight—the sum total of which makes up 'our (life), our cosmic organism'. For it is there that God must lie hidden. . . .

Here again, cannot *the object, the actual matter* of our human passions be transfigured, transformed into the Absolute, the definitive, the divine?—I believe it can. . . . I shall divinize the ingenuous or inquisitive love of nature, by considering that something of this mysterious whole represented by Matter, must pass through Resurrection, pass into the World of heaven—my efforts to forward human progress being even (??perhaps) the necessary condition for the development of the new Earth.—And so, with not break, carried along by the natural graduated advance of the material, the living, the social, I find at the term of my desires the 'cosmic Christ' (if I may use the phrase), he who gathers together at the conscious Center of his Person and his Heart, every movement of atoms, cells, souls . . .

That is what I vaguely see, and am trying to bring out. . . . I would like to be able to love Christ passionately (*by* loving) *in the very act* of loving the universe. Is it a wild dream or a blasphemy? Besides communion with God and communion with the Earth, is there communion with God through the Earth—the Earth becoming like a great Host in which God would be contained for us? . . . I would like that to be true (for my own sake and for that of many

others . . .)—In any case I enjoy noting down my ideas in this direction—subject to having, if need be, to add at the end, 'and that was
all a dream'.[15]

Among these many others, we too would like Teilhard's
"dream" to be, in fact, a sure glimpse of the most profound
reality. If we want to be convinced of this, however, we must
adopt intellectual honesty as well as his faith, and foster in ourselves
his passion for seeing things from the ground up.[16] Then we
must travel with him through the long and somewhat laborious
night of searching and synthesizing that led to the integrated
mysticism of co-creative union which we examine in the last
chapter. The first chapter, in which we attempt to trace in broad
sweeping lines the development of Teilhard's scientific theory,
and perhaps even parts of the second chapter, in which we delve
into his theological premises, may seem especially laborious to
readers not acquainted with Teilhard's terminology. We hope
that the simple glossary included at the end of the preface will
help through any thickets, but we are convinced that those who
are seeking the deeper and more integrated spirituality which
Teilhard proposes, will welcome the opportunity to probe the
scientific as well as the theological foundation on which he based
his spirituality. For in the words of Henri de Lubac, "a spirituality can be understood and judged only in its relation to the sum
total of the truths on which it is based." [17] The milestones along
our way seem clearly marked for us by the concise equation-
summary of his system which Teilhard entered into his diary on
the Good Friday before his death:

Cosmos = Cosmogenesis – Biogenesis – Noogenesis – Christogenesis.[18]

[15] Letter of March 15, 1916, in de Lubac, *The Religion* . . ., pp. 243-244.
[16] Claude Cuénot, *Teilhard de Chardin* (Baltimore: Helicon, 1965), p. 107.
[17] Henri de Lubac, *The Religion* . . ., p. 19.
[18] Entry in Diary, April 7, 1955, quoted by French Editor at the Conclusion of P. Teilhard de Chardin, *The Future of Man* (New York: Harper
and Row, 1964), p. 309, hereafter cited as *FM*.

CHAPTER ONE

The Humanized Labor of Cosmogenesis

The Field of Human Labor:
A Cosmogenesis Propelled by the
Law of Complexity/Consciousness

Teilhard provides the key to his thought on human labor, as well as the direction of our present study in the following extract from his essay, "Research, Work and Adoration."

A Christian appraisal of work can only be possible, I think, if we start from an outlook (*Weltanschaung*) that stresses the relation between Arrangement of Matter and Christification: or, if you prefer, from establishing a certain relation between cosmogenesis, anthropogenesis, and Christogenesis.[1]

Our focus is on man. How can his labor have any significance in a world of evolution? If, as we shall see, man is rooted so very firmly in the "stuff" of the world and seems to emerge as just one more stage of cosmogenesis passively borne along in some sort of development due to mysterious cosmic forces, what significance can *he* have, let alone his work? As a preview, Teilhard's answer will be what he calls a "neo-anthropocentricism of movement" which postulates man as "no longer the center, but an arrow shot towards the center of the Universe in process of concentration." [2]

[1] "Research, Work and Adoration," *Oeuvres* IX, quoted in Cuénot, p. 374.
[2] "The Singularities of the Human Species," in P. Teilhard de Chardin, *The Appearance of Man* (New York: Harper and Row, 1965), pp. 209-10, hereafter cited as *AM*. See also P. Teilhard de Chardin, *The Phenomenon of Man* (New York: Harper Torchbooks, 1961), p. 223, hereafter cited as *PM*.

But as we have already indicated, to understand what he means and to lay the foundations of his spirituality, we must start, as he did, at the beginning.

Using the laws discerned in that part of the evolutionary process that lies within the range of man's scientific observation, the scientist can reconstruct hypothetically the stages that preceded it, and even postulate a theory regarding the nature of the world's beginnings. Teilhard, speaking scientifically, and here interpreted in a quite free and non-technical "translation," proposes that the world began with some sort of primordial energy appearing right from the start in a granulated form. This energy began at once to break up rapidly into "swarms of elements" which would become "the positive, negative and natural elements of the atom." Then, through the interaction of cosmic forces these elements began to come together in increasingly complex and centered arrangements (atoms), which in turn grouped together in more complex arrangements, and so on, repeating this process and causing the slow evolution of matter into the world of persons which we live in today. As the arrangements of matter at any given stage grouped together, they would be pressured by their greater complexity to rearrange themselves in a higher synthesis having a greater degree of centrating power to control this more complex arrangement. The centering or synthesizing force of each new arrangement Teilhard calls its consciousness, even though this primitive psychism or "within" of things was a dim foreshadowing of the consciousness that would emerge with the development of animal nervous systems. As the centrating power or consciousness increased at each new stage of complexity, it would reach out, as it were, to join together with equally complex and centered arrangements, merging with them to form an ever more tightly centered complexity. Evolution continues, therefore, along a single axis of increasingly more centered arrangements, impelled by a double, inter-causal force of complexity/consciousness, which is the law governing the whole of evolution.[3]

[3] "The Singularities of the Human Species," *AM*, pp. 211-219.

In the process of evolving, matter reaches its optimum degree of complexity and consciousness beyond which it cannot be "pushed." At this "critical point" the excess of psychic energy explodes, as it were, into a new, freer sphere where there are possibilities for centered arrangements of a higher order. The first major critical point of evolution caused the "birth" of life, and into the new biosphere rushed the full might of the evolutionary drive; cosmogenesis became biogenesis. In the biosphere the energy of complexity/consciousness finds expression in the development of the brain and nervous systems of animal organisms, a process called cerebration which allows the scientist to trace the progress of biogenesis toward its optimum point of consciousness.[4] This critical point coincides with what Teilhard calls "some 'inspired' trick of connexion and arrangement in the neurons of the brain," a "neurophysical 'mutation';"[5] or, in simple terms, some change occurs by chance in the physical structure and arrangement of the nervous system, and at that precise instant the brain becomes capable of reflective thought or "consciousness raised to the power of two."[6] Thus man was born, a reflective center of synthesis and self-determination; and in him evolution became conscious of itself and capable of directing its own progress.[7] Once again the evolution energy rushes into this new sphere, comprising the human phylum, where the possibilities of "a particular type of organo-social arrangement,"[8] that is, of "planetisation," will enable the cosmos-in-evolution, now raised from biogenesis to the level of noogenesis, to reach a new and final optimum or critical point, in the hyper-co-reflection of a super-personalizing spiritual union.

"In man, fantastically enough, the whole of evolution rebounds on itself"; "it is interiorised and made purposeful."[9]

Below this critical point everything happens (perhaps?) as though the

[4] Ibid., pp. 215, 222.
[5] Ibid., pp. 211, 226, footnote 2.
[6] Ibid., p. 224.
[7] Ibid., p. 254; PM, p. 220.
[8] "The Singularities of the Human Species," AM, p. 224.
[9] Ibid., p. 227; "The Human Rebound of Evolution," FM, p. 212.

rise of Life were automatic. But above it the forces of free choice and inner direction come to light and it is they that tend to take charge.[10]

In man the force of evolution becomes the "force of purposive thinking"; and we see the human phylum, and thus the whole cosmos, "passing from the normal regime of passive evolution to that of self-guided evolution." Now, if the drive of complexity/consciousness is to progress towards higher syntheses, it can do so only through the reflective and, higher still, co-reflective syntheses of human thought; and if such progress in consciousness demands as its prerequisite a certain degree of complexity in material arrangement, that complexity will only be achieved by the deliberate activity of man, organizing matter or socially arranging himself. Man has truly become the "arrow shot towards the center of the Universe in process of concentration" [11] and drawing in its wake the entire cosmos. It is an arrow, however, that however passively it was shot, can only continue and reach its mark by becoming increasingly self-propelled; or more precisely, man must deliberately foster within himself, both individually and collectively, the vital energy of cosmogenesis. This he does, quite simply, by thinking—thinking deeply and honestly, energetically and creatively—and together. Proceeding through the space-time cone of evolution, along the one same axis of complexity/consciousness, though now at the incomparably higher degree of incandescence of the noosphere, mankind moves ineluctably along a path of growing socialization and self-understanding, developing a variety of civilizations, and reaching, today, the threshold of some hyper-socialization or planetization and the formation of a single civilization.[12]

After the break-through of reflection, men, in the first flush of self-centeredness and autonomy, tended to spread out and expand over the globe. Counteracting this tendency, their growth in numbers and the naturally compressing roundness of the globe necessitated forming themselves in socio-politico-economic groupings which, in turn, by the co-reflection this engendered,

[10] "The Human Rebound of Evolution," *FM*, p. 200.
[11] *PM*, p. 223; "The Singularities of the Human Species," *AM*, pp. 209-10.
[12] "The Singularities of the Human Species," *AM*, pp. 246-6; "The Phyletic Structure of the Human Group, *AM*, pp. 158-9.

caused an increased self-awareness and its expression in culture and technology. This latter led to more complex social arrangements, which engendered a more refined culture and technology, and so the spiralling progress of mankind has continued to the present day. Today, the population explosion and rapid advances in technology, particularly in the communications media, have brought increased "pressure" to bear on man's efforts to interpenetrate and unite in an increased co-reflection. Corresponding to this more spiritualized complexity of modern civilization is the coming to bud (the flower may be long in blooming!) of a common vision of the world, and a "sense of earth"—"the passionate concern for our common destiny which draws the thinking part of life ever further onward." [13] In spite of world crises which would seem to prove the contrary, we are, Teilhard assures us, on the threshold of a new era of ultra-socialization when, having broken down the barriers of nationalisms, of individual and collective egoisms, and with heightened powers of co-reflection operating "in a world constantly more orderly and better understood," [14] we will unite in a common vision and a common passion to build the earth. Then, with constantly accelerating speed, cosmogenesis-become-noogenesis will coil in on itself until it reaches its term. Its final critical point, if it is not a dead end, can only be some kind of ultra-personalizing paroxysm of co-reflection.[15]

It is just inside this threshold of the new age, the age of the ultra-human, the co-reflective, that modern man is awakening to the dizzying awareness "both of the general evolutionary tendency of which he forms (in the field of our experience) the supreme point, and of the power conferred on him of influencing or even guiding this current." [16] "He feels in himself the responsibility and the power of an entire Universe." [17]

[13] "The Planetization of Mankind," FM, p. 132; "L'esprit de la terre," L'énergie humaine, Oeuvres VI, p. 23. Cf. Teilhard de Chardin, Man's Place in Nature (New York: Harper and Row, 1966), pp. 79-112, hereafter cited as MPN.

[14] "The Singularities of the Human Species," AM, p. 244.

[15] PM, pp. 287-9; see also: AM, pp. 169-70, 258, and FM, pp. 198, 264.

[16] "The Phyletic Structure of the Human Group," AM, p. 164.

[17] "A Note on Progress," FM, p. 18.

It is mankind as a whole, collective humanity, that is called upon to perform the definitive act whereby the total force of terrestrial evolution will be released and flourish; an act in which the full consciousness of each individual man will be sustained by that of every other man, not only the living but the dead. And it follows that the *opus humanum* laboriously and gradually achieved within us by the growth of knowledge and in the face of evil, is something quite other than an act of higher morality: it is a living organism. We cannot distinctly view its progress because the organism encloses us, and to know a thing synthetically one has to be in control of it.[18]

The great work of man, therefore, upon which the whole success of evolution depends, is to achieve something within himself, collectively; it is to construct the psychological organism of the Noosphere, the collective, spiritual "Brain" and "Heart" of Mankind totalized and personalized in absolute unity—somehow. And the whole meaning and grandeur of human work lies in just this: that it is the essential condition for the progress of cosmogenesis to its term—which at this point in our journey is still unknown. "Progress, if it is to continue, will not happen by itself." [19] It will happen through us, or it will not happen at all.

At once humbled and ennobled by our discoveries, we are gradually coming to see ourselves as a part of vast and continuing processes; as though awakening from a dream, we are beginning to realize that our nobility consists in serving, like intelligent atoms, the work proceeding in the universe. We have discovered that there is a Whole of which we are the elements. We have found the world in our souls.[20]

But we cannot just bask in the glory of our new-found importance; there is work to do!

Research and Invention:
The Means of Humanizing and Furthering Cosmogenesis

From the moment that we realize our heavy cosmic responsibility, "our perfection, our interest, our salvation as elements of creation can only be to press on with this evolution with all our

[18] *Ibid.*, p. 20.
[19] "Réflexions sur le progrès," *L'activation de l'énergie, Oeuvres* VII, pp. 27-63.
[20] "A Note on Progress," *FM*, pp. 16-17. See also *PM*, p. 180.

strength." [21] The key work of man which furthers cosmogenesis is research, which progresses correlatively with socialization and technology. If "the spirit of research and conquest is the permanent soul of evolution," [22] it is because it is no more nor less than the consequence of complexity/consciousness operating in its noospheric state. It is "in the simultaneous rise of Society, the Machine and Thought" that we discern the "primordial process of Life itself . . . whereby ever-increasing unity, accompanied by ever-heightened awareness, is achieved by ever more complicated structural arrangements." [23] The more man intelligently organizes matter by technology for the service of mind, the freer he is to think. Likewise, the better he organizes himself in society, the surer he is to interpenetrate, to think together, synthetically, and to achieve a heightened co-reflection. In fact, the "crown of evolution" is actually "a supreme act of collective vision obtained by a pan-human effort of investigation and construction." [24] All work, therefore, is for Thought; we labor collectively, fulfilling a variety of necessary but insufficient functions, so that together we may know—and ultimately, so that knowing we may come together in love and fullness of vision.

Essentially progress is a *force* . . . It is the consciousness of all that is and all that can be . . . to *be* more is in the first place to *know* more. Hence . . . to be faithful to life we must *know;* we must know more and still more; we must tirelessly and unceasingly search for Something, we know not what, which will appear in the end to those who have penetrated to the very heart of reality.[25]

In fact, considering that the whole evolutionary force in biogenesis concentrated "in the direction of the largest brain," Teilhard observes, "we are compelled to wonder whether the true fundamental impulse underlying the growth of animal forces has not been the need to know and think." [26] Similarly, Teilhard sees the modern phenomenon of technological progress as a great planetary and noospheric cerebration, the formation of that "Brain of

[21] "L'énergie humaine," *L'énergie humaine, Oeuvres* VI, pp. 141-2.
[22] *PM*, p. 223.
[23] *PM*, p. 249.
[24] "A Note on Progress," *FM*, pp. 19-20.
[25] "The Formation of the Noosphere," *FM*, p. 166.
[26] "The Directions and Conditions of the Future," *FM*, p. 231.

brains" [27] with which mankind can progress through ever more tightening degrees of co-reflection towards the fullness of light and synthesis.

Now, can we fail to recognize in the enormous and incredibly complicated system of modern technico-social mechanization the authentic and direct continuation of the biological action and the process of cerebration?

Yes, ever and again, cerebration, the main axis of zoological evolution, in the form of collective research. But this time a cerebration carried by extreme compression, to the level of the Noosphere. And what is still more remarkable, a cerebration henceforth endowed with the entirely new power of foreseeing and planning its own developments.[28]

If this is so, may we not expect that the climax of noospheric cerebration would also be analogous to that "neurophysical nutation" [29] that marked the biosphere's critical point and the birth of reflection? And wouldn't it be just this "'inspired' trick" [30] of complexity that man's efforts in technology and socialization, simultaneously the products and the conditions of increasing collective research, must in growing measure foresee and plan?

Let that man take heart, then, whether inventor, craftsman, or common laborer, whose every day is consumed in a kind of immersion in matter that seems to reduce him to an impersonal nonentity, particularly in assembly-line types of manufacture.[31] Each is furthering Noogenesis whenever he contributes, however infinitesimally, to the construction or operation of machinery: not only "the machine which liberates, relieving both individual and collective thought of the trammels which hinder its progress, but also the machine which creates, helping to assemble, and to concentrate in an ever more deeply penetrating organism, all the reflective elements upon earth." [32] From the humblest primitive

[27] "The Formation of the Noosphere," *FM*, p. 166.
[28] "The Phyletic Structure of the Human Group," *AM*, p. 163.
[29] "The Singularities of the Human Species," *AM*, p. 211.
[30] *Ibid.*, p. 226, footnote 2.
[31] Marcel van Caster, S.J., "Human and Christian Meaning of Work," a reprint from *Lumen Vitae* 22 (1965), pp. 25-30.
[32] "The Formation of the Noosphere," *FM*, p. 167.

tool up to the most complex electronic computers, it is the machine which not only frees us for, but assists us in thinking; for it

both facilitates and indefinitely multiplies our activities. Not only does it relieve us mechanically of a crushing weight of physical and mental labor; but by the miraculous enhancing of our senses, through the powers of enlargement, penetration and exact measurement, it constantly increases the scope and exact measurement of our perceptions. It fulfills the dream of all living creatures by satisfying our instinctive craving for *the maximum of consciousness* with a minimum of effort! Having embarked upon so profitable a path, how can Mankind fail to pursue it? [33]

Mankind might be tempted to give up the pursuit of this growing mechanization in the face of that distressing phenomenon of our day, unemployment. Yet, however much we must deplore man's failure to prepare, by proper education, for this partially foreseen crisis, we are forced to acknowledge that, examined in the light of the complexity/consciousness law, it is a necessary step in the progress of Noogenesis. Unemployment has released a prodigious amount of psychic energy which we need only to harness and direct by education in order to see a great flourishing of collective research. The age of technology must inevitably lead to the age of research.[34] In spite of the problems which today's transitional age must face because of unemployment, to try to block the technological progress which caused it would be to attempt to prevent the progress of the "most irresistible power in the universe . . . a drift of matter towards an order that will allow it increasing interiorization." [35] We need only to stand back and view our age from a higher vantage point to realize that innumerable "jobs" are waiting to be filled first of all by those who are willing to work towards the solution of the problems of unemployment by directing mankind towards research; and then, by those who are willing to dedicate themselves to that research

[33] "The Directions and Conditions of the Future," *FM*, pp. 167, 229-30.
[34] "The Formation of the Noosphere," *FM*, pp. 171-3; *PM*, pp. 252-3; cf. *MPN*, pp. 104-107.
[35] "The Phyletic Structure of the Human Group," *AM*, p. 161.

in the new and almost fantastic fields of endeavor that are opening up before them.

For the man who gives himself to the more exalted (and more demanding) work of creative research, there is the greatest possibility of realizing Teilhard's conviction that

the substantial joy of life is found in the consciousness, or feeling, that by *everything* we enjoy, create, overcome, discover, or suffer, in ourselves or in others, in any possible line of life or death (organic, biological, social, artistic, scientific, etc.) we are increasing (and we are gradually incorporated into) the growing Soul or Spirit of the world.[36]

In a letter written in 1933 Teilhard exalted the role of the scientist even further, giving him much needed encouragement for his exhausting and often "blind" labors, analogous to those blind gropings of pre-reflective matter for arrangement and synthesis which were no doubt the most primitive forerunners of research.[37] He writes:

You ask yourself: 'Is scientific research a derivation or a deviation?' —I think that it is one form (one of the most perfect, of the most direct) of what we call being, or life, or Evolution. I cannot define the World otherwise than by a gradual awakening of consciousness: research is precisely the frontier in the spreading of this universal consciousness. Thus, the question of the value of our efforts is solved. Our efforts have the same value as the Universe which atomically develops itself in each one of us. It all comes back to accepting the hypothesis that the Universe is neither a negligible nor an absurd thing—and that as a consequence it is satisfying (or even beautifying) to be entrusted to that which develops itself in each of us.[38]

The frontier in the spreading of universal consciousness—the arrow*head*—such is the essential dignity and function of research; it forms the front lines in the advance of Noogenesis and the formation of man's collective "Brain." To accomplish this objective, man must focus his research not only on the subhuman level of matter, seeking to draw the whole material world,

[36] From a short profession of faith written in English, Sept. 28, 1933, in Cuénot, p. 217.
[37] *PM*, p. 223.
[38] Cuénot, p. 217, footnote 10.

potentially mankind's cosmic body, into the service and synthesis of Thought, as we have seen.[39] He must focus his inventiveness also, and more importantly, on himself, perfecting as far as possible his own thinking apparatus; and finally, on an even higher level, his efforts must center on education and on the politico-economic social structures which can foster the unanimization essential for the growth of collective thought.

Having made such great strides in mechanization on the sub-human level, man today is awakening, through the merging efforts of many relatively new sciences, to an exciting yet rather frightening prospect. The most crucial matter to subject to Thought is the human brain itself. Noogenesis is contigent upon the reflective perfection of each thinking element.

The first object which should attract the attention of the technician of human energy is to ensure to the human nuclei taken in isolation, their maximum of consistency and efficiency as elements. To perfect individuals so as to confer upon the whole the maximum of power [knowledge for power . . . increased power for increased action . . . increased action for increased being],[40] that is the obvious line to follow for the final success of the operation.[41]

In the new era of science that we are fast approaching, therefore, "Man, the knowing subject, will perceive at last that man, 'the object of knowledge,' is the key to the whole science of nature." [42] This new man-centered science will involve, for one thing, the expansion of efforts already being made in the field of conservation, particularly food production and distribution. "To think we must eat." [43] With population rising and arable land decreasing, science must devote serious attention to the problem of feeding mankind.

Where physical energy and even organic substance are concerned, science can foresee and indeed already possesses inexhaustible substitutes for coal, petroleum and certain metals. But foodstuffs are an-

---

[39] "A Note on Progress," *FM*, p. 17; "The Formation of the Noosphere," *FM*, p. 177.
[40] *PM*, p. 249.
[41] "L'énergie humaine," *L'énergie humaine, Oeuvres* VI, p. 159.
[42] *PM*, pp. 280-81.
[43] *PM*, p. 63.

other matter. How long (if it ever happens at all) will it take chemical science to find ways of feeding us by the direct conversion of carbon, nitrogen and other simple elements? . . . We must take care: we still have feet of clay.[44]

A more direct way, of course, of ensuring the progress of the individual man is "the care and improvement of the human body, the health and strength of the organism."[45] Within this area of research, today, it is a question "less of hygiene and physical culture, to which sufficient thought is devoted already, than of the vital problems posed by genetics, which are willfully ignored."[46] If, as we have seen, the noogenesis which research effects amounts to a noospheric cerebration, the most vital area of attack for that research must be the actual physical perfection of the individual human brain, first of all, and then, secondly, the perfection of the physical arrangement of the collective brain—including, in both cases, a nervous system. Is it possible that man could perfect his own brain?

Following the convergent paths of genetics, biochemistry, endocrinology, cerebrology, and the new psychology, man associated with all other men, feels that the hour is fast approaching when, forced by his own destiny, he will succeed in putting his finger on the most basic springs of his own organic development.[47]

This means, quite simply, that he will "succeed in one day perfecting his own nervous system";[48] which would mean that he would control anthropogenesis in "its most axial and active *germ*."[49] The thought that one day, perhaps not so far distant, man will "lay his hands so efficaciously on the mechanism of reproduction, embryogenesis and selection that not only the social group taken in its global form, but individuals themselves, from generation to generation will be increasingly *cerebralized*,

[44] "The Directions and Conditions of the Future," *FM*, p. 233.
[45] *PM*, p. 282.
[46] *FM*, p. 233.
[47] "The Phyletic Structure of the Human Group," *AM*, p. 164.
[48] "The Singularities of the Human Species," *AM*, p. 254; cf. *MPN*, pp. 110-112.
[49] "The Phyletic Structure of the Human Group," *AM*, p. 164.

not only by natural selection but by *directed* selection"—without a doubt, this does seem to be a "fantastic" prospect, a "wild imagination," but it is one that is beginning "to be viewed quite seriously." The many "objections of head and heart, of morality and religion" which the prospect of possessing, and even worse, of acquiring such a power raise are valid and serious.[50] We can only hope that mankind's growth in morality, based on progress in "personalization" and "unanimization" through love (a factor of noogenesis we have yet to consider), will keep pace with his scientific advancement. Then, we can anticipate "a nobly human form of eugenics, on a standard worthy of our personalities";[51] for "(whether we like it or not) let us finally realize," Teilhard says, "that nothing, absolutely nothing will ever prevent man (driven to it as he is by an inner urge of cosmic nature) from going *in every direction*—and more especially in the biological field—*to the utmost extent* of his powers of research and invention."[52]

Closely related to eugenics, by its function to perfect the individual thinker in his reflective power as well as in his possession of the collective body of knowledge, is education. Perhaps even more than the eugenist, it is the educator who has his finger on the "most axial and active"[53] principle of anthropo- (hence cosmo-) genesis. It is education which forms the continuing and inseparable matrix of the collective consciousness of mankind, the matrix, therefore, of the very "stuff" of the noosphere, and of the spiritual "Brain" and nervous system of humanity. As the mechanism replacing heredity, education is the very mainspring of noogenesis, transmitting and furthering the organic progress of reflective complexity/consciousness in the shape of mankind's collective memory.[54] Now it is the educator's turn to take heart! Only by advancing the excellence and the universality of our

[50] "The Singularities of the Human Species," *AM*, p. 254.
[51] *PM*, p. 282.
[52] "The Singularities of the Human Species," *AM*, p. 255.
[53] "The Phyletic Structure of the Human Group," *AM*, p. 164.
[54] "Social Heredity and Progress," *FM*, pp. 26-32; *PM*, pp. 178, 224-5; "The Singularities of the Human Species," *AM*, pp. 242-4.

education, leading man to ever more penetrating research and a heightened collective vision, shall we see the fulfillment of Teilhard's prediction: "It will not be long now before the noosphere finds its eyes." [55]

Collective Research:
The Means of Progressing toward Planetization

No degree of progress in the perfecting of man individually and collectively, however, will of itself ensure the successful outcome of noogenesis; nor would that progress even be possible, were it not accompanied by a correlative growth of unanimization, that is, of the personal union of mankind in love. This fact (which remains yet to be examined in the present study) points to the necessity of an increasingly collective dimension of any research that is to meet the progressive demands of noogenesis. It also directs our attention to the highest object of that research, mankind as a whole, as well as to a branch of science that might be called a "eugenics applied to society." [56] Further, it will lead us to the personalist center of the axis of noogenesis at the innermost heart of the noosphere.

It is the basic law of complexity/consciousness which demands that our research, if it is to progress and lead to ever greater heights of co-reflection, must become increasingly a collective effort, permeated by a team spirit. Only an increasingly complex inter-penetration and inter-action of "reflective centers" can give birth to that super-consciousness or hyper-co-reflection required for the unanimity of vision which is evolution's ultimate goal. It is, in short, a team of brains that is essential for the construction of the noospheric "Brain of brains"; only such an integrated research team will be capable of achieving, or rather spearheading mankind's achievement of that collective synthesis which erects, "as though it were a vault above our heads, a domain of interwoven consciousness, the site, support and instru-

[55] *PM*, p. 280.
[56] *PM*, p. 282.

ment of super-vision and super-ideas." [57] Probably the most familiar illustration of this is the NASA space team, whose awesome, hypercomplex network of interacting intelligences, supported by a parallel maze of interacting machinery, has achieved such feats in man's collective conquest of outer space. Less perceptible, yet even more real and significant, is the vast interreacting web of philosophic thought by which mankind is growing up in its own self-understanding (not escaping, we might add, a series of "identity crises" alluded to by Teilhard).[58]

We have only to consider any of the new concepts and intuitions which, particularly during the last century, have become or are in the process of becoming the indestructible keystone and fabric of our thought—the idea of the atom, for example, or of organic Time or Evolution. It is surely obvious that no man on earth could alone have evolved them; no one man, *thinking by himself*, can encompass, master or exhaust them; yet every man on earth shares *in himself*, in the universal heightening of consciousness promoted by the existence in our minds of these new concepts of matter and new dimensions of cosmic reality.[59]

We note that the individual is not lost but enhanced by the fruits of collective research; he is the rich heir of a collective vision which he never could have seen by himself. He has a responsibility by this very fact, however, to strain his own small powers of reflection to their limits to contribute to this common treasure, not disheartened but elated that it is something beyond his own limits that he is helping to produce. "No doubt everything proceeds from the individual," Teilhard concludes, "and in the first instance depends on the individual; but it is on a higher level than the individual that everything achieves its fulfillment." [60]

Not only is the highest form of research collective in its operation; it is also collective in its object. From man's earliest days, it has been progress in social grouping, more or less haphazard at first, and circumstantially required for existence, that led to the beginnings of co-reflection and the development of civiliza-

[57] "The Formation of the Noosphere," *FM*, pp. 168-9.
[58] "The New Spirit, 1942," *FM*, p. 86.
[59] "The Formation of the Noosphere," *FM*, pp. 168-9.
[60] *Ibid.*, p. 169.

tions—an effect of the fundamental law of complexity/consciousness, as we saw at the beginning of this study. Today, in this dawning era of self-evolution, certainly the best of our efforts should be applied to arranging the most noospherically fruitful social groupings, from the smallest seminar group to the United Nations. This "eugenics applied to society," as Teilhard calls it,[61] would involve an international research and cooperation in such earth-building socio-politico-economic activities as: the distribution of the resources of the globe; the control of the trek towards unpopulated areas; the optimum use of the powers set free by mechanization; the physiology of nations and races; geo-economy; geo-politics; geo-demography; the organization of research developing into a reasoned organization of the earth.[62] Let those who are pessimistic about the resolution of the unemployment problem take note. Certainly there is a wide field of labor opening before us, if we will only prepare ourselves: a multitudinous variety of jobs awaiting those who are willing to dedicate themselves to the team effort of constructing, through the "super-complexification" of humanity and its consequent "super-interiorization," the body and the true home "of the *Man* who is to be born tomorrow." [63] An area of technology that is particularly related to man's efforts towards planetization is one we have already noted, the communications media. "The extraordinary network of radio and television communications, which, perhaps anticipating the direct inter-communication of brains through the mysterious power of telepathy, already link us all in a sort of 'etherized' universal consciousness." [64] This progressively more refined inter-communication system will be, perhaps, the principal tool of the "social eugenists."

The social mechanization, as it were, of mankind is probably the most crucial work of our times, if our age is to fulfill its historical task in the progress of cosmogenesis. The critical hour

[61] *PM*, p. 282.
[62] *PM*, p. 283.
[63] "Does Mankind Move Biologically Upon Itself?" *FM*, p. 254.
[64] "The Formation of the Noosphere," *FM*, p. 167.

for planetization, the moment of decision, is now. "We cannot wait passively upon the statistical play of events to decide for us which road the world is to take tomorrow. We must positively and ardently take a hand in the game ourselves." [65] Since we are "borne on a current of Totalisation that is taking shape and gathering speed around us, we cannot," Teilhard insists, "either stop or turn back." [66] If we are going to move forward, and this is the only direction in which we *can move*, we must intelligently and courageously harness the force of planetization and steer the "super-organisation of the world" in the direction of a super-personalizing union, which is the only direction that lies *ahead*.[67] And once having made the choice of "human totalisation," then no matter how "politically, economically, and psychologically obscure" the faint horizon of this planetized humanity of the future remains, and no matter how difficult the efforts are to reconcile the political ideologies and forces which we see confronting each other today and struggling for possession of the earth, we must remain optimistic about the future of our world.[68] "How can we lay down limits to the effect of expansion, penetration and spiritual fusion which would flow from the coherent ordering of our human multitude?" [69] It is the optimistic "toilers of the Earth" who "will tomorrow constitute the human race"; it will be through their labor that mankind will have at last entered into "its *sympathetic phase* under the influence of the newly manifest Sense of Evolution." [70] To this "sympathetic phase," the ultimate in socialization, we must turn our attention now, if we would follow the in-coiling evolutionary "vortex" to its end point and note the correspondingly more spiritual activity required of man to effect this in-coiling.[71]

[65] "Does Mankind Move Biologically Upon Itself?" *FM*, p. 256.
[66] *Ibid.*, p. 255.
[67] *Ibid.*, pp. 253-9.
[68] *Ibid.*, p. 259, footnote 1. Cf. "Sauvons l'humanité," *Science et Christ*, Oeuvres IX, p. 169.
[69] "L'énergie humaine," *L'énergie humaine, Oeuvres* VI, p. 165.
[70] "The Planetization of Mankind," *FM*, p. 138.
[71] "The Singularities of the Human Species," *AM*, p. 238.

Love:
The Ultimate Energy of Cosmogenesis,
the Power of Unanimization

It is not enough that we should set about constructing the cosmic body of a future ultra-humanity; we must also labor to become its soul.[72] The term of noogenesis towards which we are striving is not merely a collectivity of workers, however necessary such a collectivity is for progress towards it. The only possible term of reflective in-coiling can be a union of persons in a common vision of all that is, a union and a vision made possible only when co-reflection has achieved its ultimate in inter-penetration, when the personal reflective centers unite center-to-center in love. "By its very nature co-reflection cannot possibly be conceived of as indefinitely intensifying within itself without first being affected and then gradually penetrated . . . by *unanimity*."[73] In a word, we shall *see all* only when we see *as one;* and we shall see as one only when we see *from within one another.* To achieve this required unanimity, Teilhard explains, will take more than a common vision built up by our collective research, or the common action of furthering universal progress.

A common body of knowledge brings together nothing but the geometric point of intelligences. A common aspiration, no matter how ardent, can only touch individuals indirectly and in an impersonal way that is depersonalizing in itself.

It is not a *tête-à-tête* or a *corps-à-corps* that we need; it is a heart-to-heart.

. . . For, on the one hand, if the synthesis of the Spirit is to be brought about in its entirety (and this is the only possible definition of progress) it can only be done, in the last resort, through the meeting, *centre to centre*, of human units, such as can only be realized in a universal mutual love.[74]

Love is the ultimate energy, the spiritualized form of that radial or axial energy that has been the single basic drive, operating in the

---

[72] "Some Reflections on Progress," *FM*, p. 74.
[73] "The Singularities of the Human Species," *AM*, p. 256.
[74] "Some Reflections on Progress," *FM*, p. 75.

complexity/consciousness pattern, of cosmogenesis right from the beginning. "Love is the most universal, formidable and mysterious of cosmic energies"; in fact, it is "the flower of cosmic energy." [75] This, of course, would be untenable in a science that recognizes only tangible phenomena; but such a science remains at best partial. A science of "the *whole* phenomenon of man" within the evolving universe demands the recognition and integration of spirit—spiritual synthesis, spiritual energy, spiritual autonomous existence—in its scientific system.[76] Which is to say that if the science of the future is to be a science of man, a science of totalized Mankind, then it will be above all a science of love.

Love has always been carefully eliminated from realist and positivist concepts of the world; but sooner or later we shall have to acknowledge that it is the fundamental impulse of Life, or, if you prefer, the one natural medium in which the rising course of evolution can proceed. With love omitted there is truly nothing ahead of us except the forbidding prospect of standardization and enslavement—the doom of ants and termites. It is through love and within love that we must look for the deepening of our deepest self, in the life-giving coming together of humankind.

The dream which human research obscurely fosters is fundamentally that of mastering, beyond all atomic or molecular affinities, the ultimate energy of which all other energies are merely servants; and thus, by grasping the very mainspring of evolution, seizing the tiller of the world.[77]

This ultimate energy and guiding tiller can only be love.

Collectivization is inevitable.[78] "It is as impossible for Mankind not to unite upon itself as it is for the human intelligence not to go on indefinitely deepening its thought." [79] Even the most wholesale and violent anti-planetization demonstrations, which is what our world wars have amounted to, lead us to discover that

[75] "L'esprit de la terre," *L'énergie humaine, Oeuvres* VI, p. 40. "L'énergie humaine," *L'énergie humaine, Oeuvres* VI, p. 161.
[76] *PM*, p. 29.
[77] "The Grand Option," *FM*, pp. 54-5.
[78] "The Planetization of Mankind," *FM*, pp. 126-8.
[79] *Ibid.*, p. 128.

"the more we seek to thrust each other away, the more do we inter-penetrate." [80] But it is not the "doom of ants and termites" that lies ahead as the term of our progress. Planetization must be at the same time a supreme personalization or it will be nothing but a "superficial pseudo-unity" that "materializes . . . instead of spiritualizing," and "engenders no growth in consciousness." A unanimity wrought in freedom by love "alone can work the miracle of causing heightened personality to emerge from the forces of collectivity." The *true* unanimization of mankind demands

that the human units involved in the process shall draw closer together, not merely under the presssure of *external* forces, or solely by the performance of material acts, but directly, center to center, through *internal* attraction. . . . True union, the union of heart and spirit, does not enslave, nor does it neutralise the individuals which it brings together. It *super-personalises* them.[81]

This love that super-personalizes while at the same time furthering unanimization, is intensely affective and directed towards particular individuals; and at the same time it is universal, even cosmic, in scope. It is a mutual attraction borne of an awakening "human sense," [82] the discovery in one another of "a single spirit in search of itself." [83] In such a discovery we glimpse and touch, however slightly, what is most unique and incommunicable in the other, and we are mutually drawn by some mysterious and irresistible affinity towards a union that somehow fulfills us both. "To love is to discover and complete oneself in someone other than oneself"; [84] and it is love alone that is "capable of uniting living beings in such a way as to complete and fulfill them, for it alone takes them and joins them by what is deepest in themselves." [85] What is deepest is that inner point of uniqueness and incommunicability that is the essence of the personality, whose

80 *Ibid.*, p. 127.
81 "Life and the Planets," *FM*, p. 119.
82 Cuénot, p. 196.
83 "The New Spirit, 1942," *FM*, p. 92.
84 *Ibid.*
85 *PM*, p. 265.

very being is actually a mysterious relational "becoming" that seeks and achieves fulfillment in a totalizing ultra-centration in another personal center. By loving another individual we discover this deepest point in ourselves and in the other, the most vital point of our affinity; and so we experience a growing openness to all who are *other* and yet joined to us by the same affinity; at the same time we discover "the world in our souls," the world spiritualized in our collective synthesis and made the common "body" of us all, the expression, in *something* other and yet one with us all, of our personal union. Thus, when we genuinely love an individual in a center-to-center relationship, we in some measure love all mankind and the entire cosmos.[86] Animated by this "new love," therefore, which Teilhard describes as an integration of a sexual, a human, and a cosmic sense, and "without losing contact with the concrete world, the heart discovers the means of embracing them all (all *others*) together in a sentiment which preserves, despite its boundless extension, the warmth of human affection." Thus, "it becomes possible, however surprising the expression may be, to love the universe," [87] for it is a universe with "a face and a heart." [88] In fact, "a universal love . . . is the only complete and final way in which we are able to love." [89]

Also, surprising as it may seem, the age of love will emerge as the ultimate flower of the age of research. It is by working together "in the common pursuit . . . of the same truth" [90] that men will feel a growing mutual attraction and sympathy capable finally of breaking down the isolationism and even mutual repulsion that we see today hindering our progress The *tête-à-tête* and the *corps-à-corps*, therefore, are necessary preliminary *steps to* the heart-to-heart. Realizing at last that "no evolutionary future awaits man except in association with all other men," [91] individuals will find welling up within them a "Sense of Evolution," a

86 *PM*, p. 180; "The Grand Option," *FM*, p. 40.
87 Cuénot, pp. 105-6.
88 *PM*, p. 267.
89 *PM*, p. 266.
90 "The Singularities of the Human Species," *AM*, p. 256.
91 *PM*, p. 246.

"Sense of Earth," that is, a "passionate concern for our common destiny," which permeates them with an active sympathy.[92] This sympathy, flowing as it does from a deepening affective union, will effect an increased psychic inter-penetration and a more *co-operative* research, both of which will foster, in turn, a still deeper affective union. As a result of the sympathy born of collective research, "the entire complex of inter-human and inter-cosmic relations will become charged with an immediacy, an intimacy and a realism" never before experienced collectively.[93] "And it is in the depths and by the grace of this new inward sphere," characterized by "the pervasion of the human mass by the power of sympathy," that mankind "will emerge into the field of prodigious affinities." Then, having progressed already in the construction of "its composite brain," humanity will at last "find its *heart,* without which the ultimate wholeness of its powers of unification can never be fully achieved."[94] Spreading from the noospheric "heart" Teilhard sees "a flood of *sympathetic* forces" transforming the whole phenomenon of planetization:

sympathy in the first place (an act of quasi-adoration) on the part of all the elements gathered together for the general impulse that carries them along; and also the sympathy (this time fraternal) of each separate element for all that is most unique and incommunicable in each of the co-elements with which it converges in the unity, not only of a single act of vision but of a single living subject.[95]

In this world, open to the power of love and glowing with its warmth,[96] a warmth which had developed imperceptibly "beneath the icy mountain tops of speculation,"[97] a new super-research with undreamt of co-reflective powers and vision will emerge. The Sense of Earth will have at last come to men "to unite them in a common passion" to build the "new and better

[92] "The Planetization of Mankind," *FM,* p. 138; "L'esprit de la terre," *L'énergie humaine, Oeuvres* VI, p. 39.
[93] "The Formation of the Noosphere," *FM,* p. 177.
[94] *Ibid.,* pp. 177-8.
[95] "The Planetization of Mankind," *FM,* p. 135.
[96] "The New Spirit, 1942," *FM,* p. 91.
[97] "The Singularities of the Human Species," *AM,* p. 256.

body," their true cosmic home.[98] Spurred on by a common hope
—"the essential *impulse* without which nothing would be done,"
and a "passionate love of growth," and exhilarating in the fellowship of a great cosmic task, mankind will launch its full attack
against the mysteries of the world.[99] Fellowship, creative passion,
joy—these are the characteristics of that "unanimity in search
and conquest, sustained among us by the universal resolve to raise
ourselves upwards, all straining shoulder to shoulder, towards
ever greater heights of consciousness and freedom."[100] As
though anticipating a smile of amused disbelief, Teilhard hastens
to add: "If such a vista seems to us fantastic, it is simply that we
lack imagination."[101] Granted, it may be utopian to dream of
achieving this for today's world; we simply are not that far advanced in noogenesis. Teilhard does not envision the attainment
of this optimum *tomorrow!* He foresees in the rather near future
"only relative unanimity to start with; but real unity, to the
extent to which all the world is finally at one in recognizing that
the function of man is to build and direct the whole of the
earth."[102]

If we accept Teilhard's idea of a converging universe, following the lines we have developed in this paper, then the only
extrapolation we can logically make regarding cosmogenesis is
the personal union that Teilhard proposes. If evolution has moved
forward from the beginning following the law of complexity/
consciousness, it is unreasonable to suppose that the world is
suddenly going to change its most fundamental direction and
become a radically different kind of world. But the law of com-
plexity/consciousness demands that the world, having once
reached the stage of reflection, can only progress in the direction
of an optimum of co-reflection, which can ultimately be achieved

[98] "L'esprit de la terre," *L'énergie humaine, Oeuvres* VI, pp. 43-44, 46.
[99] "Reflections on Progress," *FM,* p. 72; "L'esprit de la terre, *L'énergie
humaine, Oeuvres* VI, pp. 43-46.
[100] "Faith in Peace," *FM,* p. 153.
[101] "The Human Rebound of Evolution," *FM,* p. 212.
[102] "Sauvons l'humanité," *Construire la terre,* Cahiers I (Paris: Editions du
Seuil, 1958), p. 10.

only by a communion which heightens to its optimum the reflective autonomy and incommunicability of each individual center of reflection, a hyper-personalizing union, therefore, achieved only by love. So, if we find it difficult to imagine the age of love Teilhard described, with the prodigious advances in research and invention which it produces, it is because we fail to realize the power of love, "the unlimited possibilities of intuition and interrelation which it brings." [103]

What an increase there is in his powers when, in research or in battle, Man catches the breath of affection or comradeship; what fulfillment when, in the instant of danger or enthusiasm, he finds in a flash that he has glimpsed the wonders of a kindred spirit. These faint glimmerings should help us realize what a formidable power and joy and capacity for action still slumber in the human spirit.[104]

Therefore, we need only a certain "imagination" to apply to mankind collectively the effects of love which for the most part we now experience only individually. Then we will be amazed by our realization that, however impressively complex and exacting our scientific experiments may appear, they will remain stunted and we shall not progress unless we finally learn to love one another. No wonder Teilhard, in a moment of poetic exaltation, exclaimed: "Some day after mastering the winds, the waves, the tides and gravity, we shall harness—for God—the energies of love. And then, for the second time in the history of the world, man will have discovered fire." [105]

Before we look for the ultimate source of this "fire," we must acknowledge a type of human activity that is the necessary companion of research in fanning the sparks, and that is the arts. Teilhard understandably devotes his attention to the value of science for cosmogenesis, since this was his life; but a comment he makes to his cousin Marguerite shows that he is aware also of the complementary value of the arts.

What you say about the role of music and poetry is *very true*. Those arts . . . arouse the soul *in a general way* to the search for the most

[103] "L'énergie humaine," *L'énergie humaine, Oeuvres* VI, p. 162.
[104] *Ibid.*, p. 43.
[105] Quoted on book jacket of *Building the Earth* (Wilkes-Barre, Pa.: Dimension Books, 1965).

beautiful and the greatest: they make it sensible to the whole, they *cosmicize* it, if I may use the word, sometimes by causing it to lose itself in the lower nirvana, sometimes by causing it to unite itself ardently with the great effort towards the higher spheres.[106]

The arts, in fact, seem to have a greater power of drawing the universe into the spiritual synthesis of man's vision than even the most communal and exalted research; and they are, in turn, research's first flower. Through the arts man expresses in a higher, more refined spiritual synthesis his vision of the whole to which the glimpses afforded by his research had led him. It is the artist, therefore, who extracts from matter its greatest natural power when he unites his fellow men in a supra-rational aesthetic experience of the universe, that is, when he "cosmicizes" them. The aesthetic experience is perhaps the highest natural approximation to the individual and collective totalization which love alone can ultimately achieve, and which is the ultimate goal of every man and of all mankind. To verify this, one need only recall the invigorating exaltation of his whole being, the vague yet compelling sense of renewed dedication to his work, now sensed as somehow a part of a noble universal effort towards some lofty height, the exhilarating sense of oneness with his fellow men in some higher reality, a contact with them in a common experience of a universal, of beauty, which lifted him up in joy the last time he attended a symphony, or an opera, or the ballet. If through science we synthesize the universe in our co-reflection, through the arts we incarnate it in our unanimization.[107]

Omega, Personal and Transcendent: The Ultimate Source of Love and Cause of Unanimization

Art and research, however, cannot be the ultimate cause of the love which will unite mankind, since in the final analysis it is love which energizes and sustains them. Considering the innate tendency of man towards isolationism, "the instinctive repulsion

[106] Letter of March 27, 1916, in *MM*, p. 97.
[107] Cf. Jacques Maritain, *Creative Intuition in Art and Poetry* (New York: Pantheon Books, 1955).

which as a general rule drives human beings, like molecules, away from each other," [108] what power can cause him freely to go out of himself and seek union with others? "How is this warming of hearts to be realized?" [109] This is the question that would arise most forcibly in our minds if, like Teilhard, we were not "convinced from birth" of the answer.[110] "There is but one possible way," he asserts, "in which human elements, innumerably diverse by nature, can love one another: it is by knowing themselves all to be centered upon a single 'super-center' common to all, to which they can only attain, each at the extreme of himself, through their unity." [111] If this super-center is the source and unifying focal point of personal love, it must be itself a person, and, as a center of convergence, supreme and autonomous. Also, if love is the spiritualized and personalized form of that cosmic energy that has driven evolution forward from the very beginning of time, this center must pre-exist the space-time cone of evolution; the center must be an eternal person, and the ultimate cause, because the ultimate goal, of cosmogenesis.

By the capital event of hominization the most 'advanced' part of the cosmos found itself personalized . . . Since everything in the universe, starting from Man, takes place in the personalized being, the ultimate Term of the universal Convergence must also possess (in a supreme degree) the quality of a Person. To super-animate, without destroying, a universe made up of personal elements, he must himself be a special Center.[112]

This Center Teilhard calls the Omega point, or more often, especially when referring to the *Transcendent* Center rather than to the end point of the evolution process, just Omega.

Omega is "a special Center" of convergence, capable of causing the most complete union of reflective centers while at the same time hyper-personalizing each one, because he energizes evolution by the power of a personal attraction which, once the universe becomes reflective, preserves the freedom of its personal

[108] "L'esprit de la terre," *L'énergie humaine, Oeuvres* VI, pp. 42-43.
[109] "The Directions and Conditions of the Future," *FM*, p. 235.
[110] "The Singularities of the Human Species," *AM*, p. 273.
[111] "Some Reflections on Progress," *FM*, p. 75.
[112] "L'esprit de la terre," *L'énergie humaine, Oeuvres* VI, pp. 55-56.

elements. Thus, the whole of evolution is actually a movement of the world towards personal union, in mankind, with Omega. After the birth of man the evolutionary drive behind this movement, caused by the attraction of Omega, becomes reflective and free: it becomes love. From this time on the "push" of complexity/consciousness becomes a "pull," the interior, rational invitation to personal union with Omega, a transcendent Center, supremely and universally "loving and lovable *at this very moment*." [113] It is only by a passionate desire to unite ourselves with this Center common to us all that we shall freely unite with each other, and break down, in the process, the barriers of self-centeredness which prevent our coming together. Our union, therefore, will not be one of coercion robbing us of our freedom, but one of love liberating us from a stifling egoism.

Only the eventual appearance, at the summit and in the heart of the unified world, of an autonomous center of congregation is structurally and functionally capable of inspiring, preserving and fully releasing, within a human mass still spiritually dispersed, the looked-for forces of unanimization. By this hypothesis only a veritable *super-love*, the attractive power of a veritable 'super-being,' can of psychological necessity dominate, possess and synthesize the host of earthly loves. Failing such a center of universal coherence, not metaphorical or theoretical but *real*, there can be no true union among totalized Mankind, and therefore no true substance. A world culminating in the Impersonal can bring us neither the warmth of attraction nor the hope of irreversibility (immortality) without which individual egotism will always have the last word. A veritable *Ego* at the summit of the world is needed for the consummation, without confounding them, of all the elemental *egos* of Earth.[114]

This last statement contains the root reason for the hyper-personalizing effect of union in Omega: it is not only because he attracts in a way that respects man's freedom; it is also because, by its very nature, a personal union through love, provided it is effected on a level transcending that of the individuals uniting, accentuates the uniqueness and freedom of each separate personality. Union with a transcendent, personal Center is, in fact, not

[113] "The Phyletic Structure of the Human Group," *AM*, p. 169; "Human Unanimisation," *FM*, p. 285; *PM*, p. 269.
[114] "Human Unanimisation," *FM*, pp. 286-7.

only the kind of union that would preserve the unique incommunicable substance of each person, it is the only true union possible to man in the converging cosmogenesis in which we live.

True union, the union that is produced by true progress at every stage of evolution, always differentiates.[115] When elements unite with others of the same complexity, under the force of the complexity/consciousness drive, they each become more differentiated by their new and special function within the new and higher synthesis into which they have been incorporated. "In every organized whole, the parts perfect themselves and fulfill themselves." [116] When this law is applied to reflective elements, persons, it appears all the more true. The unanimization of mankind toward which noogenesis is tending must be a union in which each reflective center, at its most unique and incommunicable core, is accentuated and perfected, or an optimum synthesis of co-reflection would be unattainable. Thus, as on every preceding level of unification effected by complexity/consciousness, men must be incorporated somehow into a new "synthesis" *higher* than themselves, which would mean, since they are persons, into a union with a supreme, transcendent Person on whom all converge and in whom each realizes personal completion. In short, at the reflective level, incorporation into a higher synthesis means incorporation into a transcendent Person.

If by the fundamental mechanism of union the elements of consciousness, drawing together, enhance what is most incommunicable in themselves, it means that the principle of unification causing them to converge is in some sort a separate reality, distinct from themselves: not a 'center of resultance' born of their converging, but a 'center of dominance' effecting the synthesis of innumerable centers culminating in itself. Without this the latter would never come together at all. In other words, in a converging Universe each element achieves completeness, not directly in a separate consummation, but by incorporation in a higher pole of consciousness in which alone it can enter into contact with all others. By a sort of inward turn

[115] *PM*, p. 262; "The Singularities of the Human Species," *AM*, p. 212, footnote 1; "The Grand Option," *FM*, p. 53.
[116] *PM*, p. 262.

toward the Other its growth culminates in an act of giving and in excentration.[117]

An "act of giving" and "excentration" is precisely what opens each "center" out to the others simultaneously as it turns them inward toward the transcendent Other; and it is this excentration, in the Other and the others, that is in reality the hyper-centration that completes the individual, totalizing him by focusing all his powers on the supreme Other, and perfecting to their ultimate all his co-reflective and affective powers. And it is precisely this act of giving and excentration that requires the actual existence and presence of a transcendent personal Center, "loving and lovable." The constant "influence of a supremely autonomous focus of union" [118] is the only adequate cause of man's uniting in love. Thus, Omega is the only conceivable motivating goal, or center, and energizing source of human unanimization—not a "deus ex machina" but the absolutely essential keystone of any coherent view of this world that is a cosmogenesis. Teilhard succinctly summarizes by stating: "For its maintenance and operation the Noosphere physically requires the existence in the universe of a real pole of psychic convergence; a Center different from all other centers, which it 'super-centers' by assimilating them; a Person distinct from all other persons, whom it fulfills by uniting them to itself." [119]

If a personal Omega is necessary for noogenesis because it is necessary for human unanimization, and if unanimization is a prerequisite for the heightened co-research of the future because it gives it an "élan vital," a Spirit of Earth, and increased psychic inter-penetration, then by the strictest logic we are drawn to the obvious conclusion that Omega is necessary for progress in research and invention, whether scientific or philosophical. And if a "loving and lovable" Omega is the ultimate condition of progress, this personal quality of Omega will probably not become an operative motivating factor on the collective level for a long time to come. An *irreversible* Omega point, however, is beginning to

[117] "The Grand Option," *FM*, pp. 55-6.
[118] *PM*, p. 262.
[119] "L'énergie humaine," *L'énergie humaine, Oeuvres* VI, p. 180.

emerge as a psychological necessity for continued labor, at least in the minds of a few men, scattered around the globe, who are imperceptibly spearheading noogenesis. "The more I examine myself," Teilhard confesses, "the more I discover this psychological truth: that no one lifts his little finger to do the smallest task unless moved, however obscurely, by the conviction that he is contributing, however infinitesimally (at least indirectly) to the construction of some absolute." [120] Regarding those who refuse to admit such a need, many of whom were no doubt his co-workers, Teilhard writes later: "What, despite all sorts of denials, sustained the most agnostic and skeptical scholars in their efforts was the obscure conviction of collaborating in a work that will never end." [121]

Progressively this "great secret preoccupation of modern man," his anxiety about the permanence of his work, must come to the fore in his consciousness. "In a planetized Humanity the *insistence upon irreversibility* becomes a specific requisite of action; and it can only grow and continue to grow as Life reveals itself as being ever more rich, an ever heavier load." [122] The reason for this is twofold. First of all, a certain *will to be* seems to underlie the forward drive of evolution, and emerges in man as a tenacious will to be *forever*.[123]

From the moment when Evolution begins to *think itself* it can no longer live with or further itself except by knowing itself to be irreversible—that is to say immortal. For what point can there be in living with eyes fixed constantly and laboriously on the future, if this future, even though it take the form of a Noosphere, must finally become a zero? [124]

Secondly, man must see that his labor is a meaningful, therefore somehow permanent, contribution to the building of a world that in him will last forever. "For the effort to push the earth forward is much too heavy, and the task threatens to go on much too long, for us to continue to accept it, unless we are to work in

[120] *DM*, p. 24.
[121] "The Singularities of the Human Species," *AM*, p. 263.
[122] "The Formation of the Noosphere," *FM*, p. 180.
[123] *Ibid.*; "The Singularities of the Human Species," *AM*, pp. 262-3.
[124] "The Human Rebound of Evolution," *FM*, p. 206.

what is incorruptible." [125] Since the world attains its culmination
in the spiritual synthesis of mankind's collective thought or vision, it is simply man himself who must be immortal for the
whole world and the fruit of all his labors to endure forever; it
endures in him as his collective, spiritual body.[126] Man's demand
for irreversibility increases as his reflective gift of foresight
makes him more and more keenly aware of two opposing ideas:
one is the possibility that evolution will terminate in some ultimate cosmic death—the paralyzing prospect of the dead end; and
the other is the necessity of his own constantly more intense
efforts if evolution is to progress.[127] The "arrow" will never
expend the tremendous energy required to draw the cosmos forward unless it becomes increasingly convinced that it has been
"shot" towards an irreversible Center, and that it will certainly
reach its mark. Man's collective labor can only be sustained,
therefore, if it is activated by a collective faith in "an ultra-center
of unification and wholeness, where there will be finally assem-
bled (in a collective synthesis), and in detail, everything that is
irreplaceable and incommunicable in the world." [128] Since this
irreversible Omega is demanded by man's *will to be forever*, by
that very fact it must be the same personal Center required for
personalizing unanimization, since in Teilhard's view the will to
be forever is synonymous with the will to be *united* forever,
while retaining, of course, one's own incommunicable being.[129]

Religion:
Achieving Union with Omega—The Problem of God

Union with Omega—how can this actually be achieved? Isn't it
really perhaps a mirage created by a desert traveler's need? If the
specter of death is to be dispelled it must be transformed into a

125 *PM*, p. 305.
126 *PM*, p. 180; "The Grand Option," *FM*, p. 40.
127 Cf. "The Grand Option," *FM*, pp. 37-60.
128 "The Formation of the Noosphere," *FM*, p. 181.
129 "Comment je vois," (unpubl.), 1948, p. 17 and note 26, quoted in
Mooney, p. 29.

vision of more being, of higher life, which is exactly what happens when death, the final cosmic death, is seen as the last critical point of evolution, the point at which the only coherent alternative to a return to multiplicity is that the universe would attain to union in Omega, and in him, to a divine synthesis. In the last year of his life Teilhard "risked" a final observation on how, following the basic law of complexity/consciousness, the universe might escape total death and emerge immortal. "The 'trick,' " he says, "consists in distinguishing two types of energies," radial and tangential. Radial or psychic energy is the primary drive of cosmogenesis, pushing forward along the axis of evolution through succeeding layers of complexity, from consciousness to consciousness, towards the peak of co-reflection. This drive of radial or axial energy is an irreversible drive, by its very nature, towards the most perfect unity of the universe in a spiritual, and necessarily personalizing (because co-reflective) synthesis. The increasingly complex arrangements of matter which the forward thrust of radial energy both causes and passes beyond are temporary phases in evolution's progress. The elements in each succeeding synthesis are held together on their own plane or level of complexity by a secondary type of energy called "tangential," which appears to be a kind of side-effect of the forward thrust of radial energy, this being, therefore, the single axial drive of evolution. Radial energy in turn seems to continuously increase due to the greater centrating pressure of each succeeding level of complexity. Tangential energy, therefore, goes the way of unorganized matter, lost to entropy. Radial energy escapes, and increasingly so at each new level of complexity, from its dependence on tangential energy, until it reaches the optimum of consciousness where it no longer needs the pressure of more complex arrangements for more centered syntheses, since it has reached the ultimate of its capacity for centration and synthesis. At this final *"critical point of super-reflexion"* there occurs "something like an emergence of co-reflexion from time and space into a definitely irreversibilized life": the "ultimate break-up of the partnership complexity/consciousness, to release, in the free state, a thinking without brain." [130] Thus, the universe appears, at least at

[130] "The Singularities of the Human Species," *AM*, pp. 264-6; *PM*, p. 51.

first glance, to escape a final death and to achieve, by the work-
ings of its own evolutionary mechanism, immortality.

Teilhard proposed this tentative scientific hypothesis as an attempt to explain how, phenomenologically speaking, cosmogenesis, following its most basic law, might achieve fulfillment in
Omega. Interesting and intellectually satisfying as the theory is, it
really doesn't adequately assure us that we *shall* ever attain such a
fulfillment. If the Omega necessary to activate noogenesis and
complete it is a pre-existent, autonomous, transcendent Omega,
that is, a Center of convergence pre-existing outside the space-
time matrix of evolution, what guarantee have we that, having
drawn the universe in man to its final critical point, Omega will
raise it above itself to personal union with himself? In Teilhard's
words, "This question may be put as follows: 'Projected as we
are towards a precise objective that lies in the future, what guarantee have we of arriving at our destination?' " [131] The very at-
tributes we have found necessary to posit of Omega make it seem
totally unreasonable to conceive of such a complete self-contradiction as an arbitrary destruction of a cosmogenesis at the moment of birth and full flowering: the self-contradiction of a "loving and lovable" transcendent Person causing "a self-abortive and
absurd universe" in which persons would experience nothing but
the deepest frustration. But we have no proof—only certain "rational invitations to an act of faith," to an option for the future
which is a *sine qua non* of our progress. Basic to these "rational
invitations" is the conviction that "in the last analysis the best
guarantee that a thing should happen is that it appears to us as
vitally necessary." [132] At the end of a lecture delivered at the
French embassy in Peking in 1945, Teilhard issued his rational
invitation to faith in the future of man with the following description of the end of the earth:

Is it not conceivable that Mankind, at the end of its totalization, its
folding-in upon itself, may reach a critical level of maturity where,
leaving Earth and stars to lapse slowly back into the dwindling mass
of primordial energy, it will detach itself from this planet and join the
one true, irreversible essence of things, the Omega point? A phenom-

[131] *MPN*, p. 117.
[132] *PM*, p. 232.

enon perhaps outwardly akin to death: but in reality a simple metamorphosis and arrival at the supreme synthesis. An escape from the planet, not in space or outwardly, but spiritually and inwardly, such as the hypercentration of cosmic matter upon itself allows.[133]

Teilhard concludes the same lecture by asserting that "this hypothesis of a final maturing and ecstasy of mankind . . . is the only one which affords a coherent prospect, wherein, in the remote future, the deepest and most powerful currents of human consciousness may converge and culminate: intelligence and action, learning and religion." [134]

And here we are, face to face with the "problem of God," and "mankind's increasingly vital need to adore." [135] Teilhard's description of the end of the earth which we just cited was preceded by two important conditions which point out the highest "work" by which man can further noogenesis.

Let us suppose that from this universal centre, this Omega point, there constantly emanate radiations hitherto only perceptible to those persons whom we call 'mystics.' Let us further imagine that, as the sensibility or response to mysticism of the human race increases with planetization, the awareness of Omega becomes so widespread as to warm the earth psychically while physically it is growing cold.[136]

A mystical awareness of Omega by a planetized mankind is the condition for the final transformation. The highest field of human endeavor, then, is clearly religion:

Religion is not an option or a strictly individual intuition, but represents the long infolding, the collective experience of all mankind, of the existence of God—God reflecting himself personally on the organized sum of thinking beings, to guarantee a sure result of creation, and to lay down exact laws for man's hesitant activities.[137]

Religion and, ultimately, mysticism are essential to noogenesis from a "strictly 'noodynamic' viewpoint," Teilhard writes to his

---

133 "Life and the Planets," *FM*, pp. 122-3.
134 *Ibid.*, p. 123.
135 "L'esprit de la terre," *L'énergie humaine, Oeuvres* VI, p. 53; *MPN*, pp. 120-121.
136 "Life and the Planets," *FM*, p. 122.
137 "L'esprit de la terre," *L'énergie humaine, Oeuvres* VI, p. 57.

scientific friends. Omega can only be the activating Center of noogenesis to the extent that man recognizes him as such and passionately desires him. He activates by the power of personal attraction. The more mankind, therefore, yields to the spiritual attraction of this Personal Center who penetrates the whole world with his influence, the more motivated and empowered it will be to progress.

Picture an earth where all men are clearly and primarily decided on advancing together to a passionately desired Being, in whom each recognizes in what was most incommunicable in his neighbor a living participation. In such a world . . . coercion would become unnecessary for the purpose of retaining individuals in the most favorable order for action. . . .[138]

For then all of man's powers of conquest, of arrangement, of synthesis will have reached their peak, totalized and focused in a single consuming act, the love of Omega.[139] And so it is that above the mechanical laborer, the technologist, above the teams of scientists or philosophers dedicated to hominization, the individual or social eugenists, above the artists who uplift and the educators who transmit, above the whole interrelated network of builders of the Earth, stand the most exalted of mankind's laborers, the men whom we might call the activating agents of the whole "noogenetic team." These are the Men of Omega, the "religionists," whose lives are devoted to fostering the most axial aspect of mankind's progress, to which we might apply Teilhard's term, "Omegalization." Among all who belong to this class the most vital are the mystics. These form the very point of the "arrow." As though finding the way ahead for us to follow, they have already pierced through the galactic darkness surrounding Omega, and in an awesome center-to-Center contact, have perceived and been transformed by those "radiations" of power, of love, which "constantly emanate" from him and permeate the universe. As their numbers increase we shall see the approach of that awesome age, probably millenniums away, in which a great collective mysticism will mark the final stage of planetization:

[138] "L'énergie humaine," L'énergie humaine, Oeuvres VI, p. 189.
[139] Ibid., pp. 182-191.

"the realization of God at the heart of the Noosphere, the apparition of the Theosphere." [140] Even today there are indications of
some movement in this direction in the "growing importance
which leading thinkers of all denominations are beginning to attach to the phenomenon of mysticism." [141]

Right from the beginning and all along the way of our journey, as we have traced the development of Teilhard's scientific
synthesis of a converging cosmogenesis and its consequent ethic
of human endeavor and mysticism, we have been vaguely conscious of a new and greater light rising on the distant horizon that
adds undreamt of richness and beauty to a landscape that even in
the moonlight had enthralled us. Now, at this height of human
mysticism, we can no longer restrain the rising sun of Christian
revelation from bursting forth and setting all the world ablaze. It
compels us to run back to the starting point once again, so that
we can retrace our steps and see all "the length and breadth and
height and depth" of human existence assumed, transformed and
consummated by a Christ-Omega. In the next chapters, therefore,
we shall trace the development and implications of Teilhard's
Christogenesis and its consequent Christian spirituality or mysticism of co-creation and co-redemption.

[140] "L'énergie humaine," *L'énergie humaine, Oeuvres* VI, p. 198.
[141] "Life and the Planets," *FM*, p. 123.

CHAPTER TWO

The Divinized Labor of Christogenesis

The Religion of the Future:
Christianity Renewed

"Who is he, sir, that may believe in him? (John 9:36)

The successful outcome of cosmogenesis, as we have seen, depends on faith, ultimately on a religious faith in a "loving and lovable" Center of universal convergence. Only a belief in a personal and transcendent Omega, giving the universe a "face" and a "heart," can activate man to plunge ahead, super-energized by the combined forces of "a passionate desire to conquer the World and a passionate longing to be united to God," which Teilhard says is "the vital act, specifically new, corresponding to a new age in the history of the Earth." [1] But to be lovable and thus inspire this "vital act," the features of the "face" and "heart" must come into focus; Omega must reveal to us his name and become present to us as a real and experienced Center, capable of drawing us into contact with himself here and now and so of constantly increasing our desire for greater union with him at the end of our labors. Being transcendent and pre-existent, Omega can only be known and experienced by us in this super-intimate way [2] if he allows some "spark" of self-revelation to leap the gap between himself and the space-time cone of his evolving world. [3] In fact, it is necessary that he himself be that spark, somehow. He

[1] "Some Reflections on Progress," *FM*, p. 81.
[2] *PM*, p. 298, footnote 1.
[3] "Esquisse d'une dialectique de l'Esprit," *Oeuvres* VII, 154. Cf. Cuénot, p. 373.

must become immersed in cosmogenesis in some way as a real and integral part, in order to become and to manifest himself as the immediate and organic Center required for the progress of noogenesis.[4]

For, in the end, however convinced we may be that a higher pole of completion and consolidation (which we may call the Omega) awaits us at the higher term of hominization, this Omega pole can never be decisively attained except by extrapolation; it will always be by its nature a conjecture and a postulate.

And this without taking into account the fact that, even if we admit that it is "guaranteed in its future existence," our anticipation of it can see only a vague, misty picture of it, in which the collective and the potential are perilously confused with the personal and the real.[5]

All the religions of the world represent man's anxious yearning to discover the features of this dimly perceived Omega, to contact him whom men instinctively have felt to be *Someone* and the Source of their being. Essentially related to this religious search is man's constant groping to understand himself within the universe, for the mysterious Omega is the key to any coherent world-view that could satisfy his need for meaning and purpose and futurity. The deep cry that arises from the depths of all of man's religious activity is simply: "Who are you, Lord? What is your name?" [6] Is there any religion that professes to have heard the answer to this cry; any religion that gives evidence, especially by its excess of love energy, of optimism, and by its dedication to progress, of having experienced contact with Omega? For, "one of the surest marks of the truth of religion, in itself and in an individual soul, is to note to what extent it brings into action, that is, causes to rise up from sources deep within us, a certain maximum of energy and effort." [7] And nowhere can we find evidence of such truth other than in Christianity. Teilhard explains:

From the strictly 'noodynamic' [spiritually energizing] viewpoint

4 Cf. "Christianisme et évolution" (unpubl.), 1945, pp. 6-7, quoted in Mooney, p. 73.
5 Cuénot, p. 372.
6 Ex. 2:13; Acts 9:5; John 9:36, 14:8.
7 Letter of July 4, 1915, *MM*, p. 58.

which I have adopted, it may be said that the historic rivalry of mysticisms and creeds, each striving to conquer the earth, represents nothing but a prolonged groping of the human soul in search of a conception of the world in which it will feel itself to be more sensitized, more free and active. This surely means that the faith which finally triumphs must be the one which shows itself to be more capable than any other of inspiring man to action. And here it is, irrespective of all philosophical and theological considerations, that Christianity decisively takes the lead with its extraordinary power of immortalizing and personalizing in Christ, to the extent of making it lovable, the time-space totality of Evolution.[8]

Before we examine the reasons behind this assertion, we might do well to glance at two major alternatives to Christianity in our world today, and also to note the religious crisis confronting our age which Christianity alone seems capable of resolving. The first alternative religion we might categorize rather generally as the ancient mysticisms, particularly of the Orient, which present themselves essentially as a method of escape from the world into some transcendent, divine sphere where the soul can rest, freed from the toil and pain and evil that imprisoned it in the world of matter. Therefore,

for almost all the ancient religions, the renewal of cosmic outlook characterizing the 'modern mind' has occasioned a crisis of such severity that, if they have not yet been killed by it, it is plain they will never recover. Narrowly bound to untenable myths, or steeped in a pessimistic and passive mysticism, they can adjust themselves neither to the precise immensities, nor to the constructive requirements, of space-time. They are out of step with our science and with our activity.[9]

For, according to the "Oriental wisdom" underlying these religions, "we must persuade ourselves of the non-existence of all surrounding phenomena, destroy the Grand Illusion by asceticism or by mysticism, create night and silence within ourselves; then at the opposite extreme of appearance, we shall penetrate to what can only be defined as a total negation—the ineffable Reality." Any deliberate "attempts to know and possess and organize

8 "The Human Rebound of Evolution," *FM*, pp. 208-9.
9 *PM*, p. 296.

the world," according to this religious belief, would be rejected as inconsistent since it would simply "strengthen the material trammels that imprison us and from which we must free ourselves if we are to attain the blessed unity." [10] The ancient religions, therefore, fail to meet Teilhard's criterion of "truth"; they are diametrically opposed to the innate sense of obligation to further human progress that forms the honest core of the modern "holy pagan," and seem destined to fade into the shadows of man's past.

The second possibility as a "true religion" is a certain neo-humanism that is arising today and that finds its rather primitive and unbalanced expression in Marxism.[11] This new "religion" of progress identifies the Omega of anthropogenesis with a materially perfected collectivization of mankind in an ultra-human state. A collectivization of this nature, however, as we noted in the first chapter, can hardly be a progression since for created persons true union can only be achieved by communion with and in a transcendent person. The Marxist type of materialistic collectivity is actually a regression for human persons as such, and as a substitute for a transcendent personal Omega is simply incapable of activating man with the hope and the love he needs to make progress.

Can Christianity do so? If it is confined and stifled by the old categories based on a static world-view, Christianity can never suranimate and divinize modern evolution-orientated paganism; but is such a world-view of the essence of Christianity? In our "God is dead" era is mankind really outgrowing Christianity along with the other ancient religions? Having glimpsed through his science a future advance of anthropogenesis toward some "terrestrial ultra-humanity" (the Marxist Omega), and feeling himself suddenly "self-sufficient and autonomous, the sole master and disposer of his destiny and the world's," modern man no longer feels any need for the "old" Christian God of the "Above" —sought and attained by despising the world and its progress. In fact, this type of Christianity is repugnant to the modern atheistic

10 "The Grand Option," *FM*, p. 43.
11 "The Heart of the Problem," *FM*, p. 264 and footnote 1.

humanist who believes in the economic and social emancipation of man and is convinced "that by its nature religion thwarts such liberation by arousing man's hope for a deceptive future life, thereby diverting him from the constructing of the earthly city." [12] This is the heart of the problem, as Teilhard sees it, of today's religious crisis with its tendency toward an anti-Christian atheism, which we must recognize as "among the most serious problems of this age." [13] It is also the source of a growing anxiety within Christians themselves, who suffer from a "religious schizophrenia," [14] a tension between their "will to love God above all else," the God of the Above, and their increasing attraction towards the "new type God ahead," that involves the perfecting of the world in man.[15] Fundamentally, it is a single religious crisis that challenges mankind today and that Christianity must confront and conquer if it is to prevail over "the gates of hell" that threaten to direct modern "neo-humanism" towards corruption; it is the same basic conflict, whether it is expressed as the professed rejection of God, that is, of "God *as in these he is represented* to Man," [16] or in the debilitating inner anxiety of the Christian. Teilhard states the problem in terms of the Above versus the Ahead:

Above or Ahead—or both? . . . This is the question that must be forced upon every human conscience by our increasing awareness of the tide of anthropogenesis on which we are borne. It is, I am convinced, the vital question, and the fact that we have thus far left it unconfronted is the root cause of all our religious troubles; whereas an answer to it, which is perfectly possible, would mark a decisive advance on the part of Mankind towards God.[16]

Teilhard suggests the direction of an answer to this question by asking another question: "The Higher Life, the Union, the long

12 "Constitution on the Church in the Modern World," art. 20, in Walter Abbott, S.J., ed. *Documents of Vatican II* (New York: America Press, 1966), p. 218.

13 *Ibid.*, art. 19, p. 216; "The Heart of the Problem," *FM*, pp. 260-3; "Faith in Man," *FM*, p. 188.

14 "Ce que le monde attend en ce moment de l'Eglise de Dieu," (unpubl.), p. 1.

15 *DM*, p. 20.

16 "The Heart of the Problem," *FM*, p. 263.

dreamed-of consummation that has hitherto been sought *Above*, in the direction of some kind of transcendency: should we not look for it *Ahead*, in the prolongation of the inherent forces of evolution?" [17]

The current religious conflict, therefore, between a static type of "Christian faith, which disdains the primacy of the ultra-human and the Earth, and 'natural' faith, which is founded upon it" [18] may actually be but the necessary step, a kind of "critical point" in mankind's religious evolution, towards a more fully human and integrated Christian faith, a faith "in God *and* the World, the one through the other." [19] A true Christian faith, " 'rectified' or 'made explicit' " in an evolutionary world-view, could reconcile both the ancient "Christian Faith, aspiring Upward," and the "Human Faith, driving Forward to the ultra-human," by focusing on Christ who, as "Savior and Mover" of anthropogenesis, is the goal of both the Upward and the Forward.[20] This reconciliation is "a necessary condition for 'tuning' Christian faith to the right frequency, and so enabling it to make the world vibrate with a new resonance." [21] But this rectifying of Christian faith can only be accomplished if the Church "embraces" what is good in the "naturally Christian soul" of the modern progressivist whose sole faith is in the perfection of man. Only then can she declare, in relevant terms, to our contemporary "men of Athens" the name of their "unknown God." This means that Christianity must discover the values of the world *below the level of God*, while inviting humanism to find room for a God above the level of this world—"the two faces of a single event which perhaps marks the beginning of a new era for Mankind." [22] Christianity's "dialogue" with the modern world, begun officially and strongly urged by the Second Vatican Council, will launch us into that new era, the last stage of our journey

[17] *Ibid.*
[18] *Ibid.*, p. 266.
[19] *Ibid.*, pp. 268-269.
[20] *Ibid.*, p. 269.
[21] Letter of May 17, 1948, in Cuénot, p. 284.
[22] "The New Spirit, 1942," *FM*, p. 96.

towards Omega, in which all of our efforts to progress will be caught up in a single Christo-centric faith and hope, a single Spirit of love: "for a faith will have been born (or re-born) containing and embracing all others—and inevitably, it is the strongest Faith which sooner or later must possess the Earth." [23]

The Church will never achieve this perfect integration of the two faiths, the Upward and the Forward, unless she renews in herself a loving awareness and faithful living out of the "double dogma on which the whole of Christianity rests, and by which it is summed up: the physical primacy of Christ and the moral primacy of charity." [24] With such a renewal Christianity will take on a "coherence and clarity" and an attracting power that it has never known before, and the light of Christ's presence will begin to penetrate more compellingly through the blinding materialism that conceals Him in the city of man.[25] The world presses us to this renewal and revitalization today more than ever before:

Never, perhaps, for two thousand years has the earth had greater need for a new faith or been more released from older forms to receive it . . . Christianity must show itself, with all its resources for renewal, now or never: God, the Christ, presenting Himself as the focus of salvation—not simply individual and 'super-natural' salvation, but collective and earth-embracing, too; and a new concept consequently of charity (incorporating and preserving the sense of the earth); and all this summed up and made concrete in the figure of the universal Christ.[26]

Thus, far from declining, Christianity alone seems capable of becoming the religion of the future. "For, by the very fact of the new dimensions assumed by the universe as we see it today, it reveals itself as inherently more vigorous in itself and as more necessary to the world than it has ever been before." [27] It gives the "crucial confirmation we are in need of" to move forward,

[23] "The Heart of the Problem," *FM*, p. 269.
[24] "The New Spirit, 1942," *FM*, p. 94.
[25] *Ibid.*, p. 93.
[26] Letter of October 18, 1940, in P. Teilhard de Chardin, *Letters from a Traveller* (New York: Harper and Row), p. 269, hereafter cited as *LT*.
[27] *PM*, p. 296.

Teilhard summarizes, "firstly by the substance of its creed [Cosmic Christ guaranteeing dynamic presence of Omega and successful outcome of cosmogenesis], next by its existence-value [flowing from its creed, a universal love actually practiced: the ultimate energy of evolution], and finally by its extraordinary power of growth [enhanced by every genuine advance in man's self-understanding]." [28] Christianity, therefore, is the most "noo-dynamic" religion for a mankind in process of evolution. Operating as a "phylum" within the human phylum, which it progressively incorporates into itself, it progresses gradually towards perfect union or personal "synthesis based on love," drawing its constant motivation and energy from an increasing consciousness of being *in actual relationship* with a spiritual and transcendent pole of universal convergence." [29] Whether the modern "believer in man" accepts Christian revelation or not—and the Church only "courteously invites atheists to examine the Gospel of Christ with an open mind" [30]—he cannot deny the historical reality of the Christian "phenomenon," and its unquestionable evidence of an incomprehensible love-power.[31] If he rejects Christ, then his is the burden of finding coherence and meaning and hope for his life elsewhere—if he can; or else he must resign himself to a frustration gnawing at the depths of his being from an awareness of being slowly "suffocated" in a universe doomed to final extinction.

If we refuse to recognize the Christian fact, we shall see the vault of the Universe, that for a moment opened above us, once again hermetically sealed.

But if we take the step, that is, if, as reasonal probability demands, we are ready to see in the living thought of the Church the reflection, adapted to our own evolutionary condition, of divine thought—then, our spirit can again move forward. And, climbing a third time [hav-

[28] *PM*, p. 296.
[29] *PM*, p. 298.
[30] "Constitution on the Church in the Modern World," art. 21, Abbott, p. 220.
[31] *PM*, pp. 292, 295.

ing arrived first at the necessity of postulating a 'transcendent Omega, the Collective Center, the Irreversible,' and secondly at the recognition of 'God the mover and revealer'] to the summit of things, we see not only some center of consistence, not only some psychic prime Mover, not even only some being that speaks, but some Word that is incarnate. If the Universe ascends progressively towards unity, it is not, then, only because impelled by some external force, but because the Transcendent has made itself to some degree immanent in it. That is what Revelation teaches us.[32]

The significance and value of Teilhard's thought for our age lies precisely in the fact that it marks out with amazing depth and breadth the way along which the Church can proceed as she rethinks and reexpresses in terms of evolution the Mystery of Christ which has been revealed to her, a way that is at once faithful to that Revelation and true to contemporary knowledge of the world. "What, when all is said and done," Teilhard writes at the end of his life," constitutes the invincible superiority of Christianity over every other type of faith is that it is becoming more and more conscious of being identified with a Christogenesis." And it is Teilhard's theory of Christogenesis that can reveal to modern man the "intense dynamic drive towards unification" that is inherent in Christianity and that derives from the three attracting "characteristics of the incarnate Christian God," tangibility, expansibility, and assimilative power, three characteristics that are placed in relief by the interrelated function that Teilhard assigns in his Christogenesis to the Incarnation, the Redemption, and the Eucharist.[33] In order to appreciate more fully the convincing correlation between the revealed Mystery of Christ conceived in terms of Christogenesis and the theory of universal evolution, and to lay the foundation for a deeper understanding of Teilhard's spirituality, we need to examine at least the main lines of the Christological synthesis that constitutes the heart of his thought.

[32] "Esquisse d'une dialectique de l'Esprit," *Oeuvres*, VII, pp. 154-155, quoted in Henri de Lubac, *Teilhard de Chardin, the Man and His Meaning*, trans. R. Hague (New York: Hawthorn Books, 1965), p. 160.
[33] "Le Christique" (unpubl.), quoted in Cuénot, p. 372.

Christ-Omega and Christogenesis

"The Lord is the goal of human history, the focal point of the longings of history and of civilization, the center of the human race, the joy of every heart and the answer to all its yearnings." [34] This statement from the conciliar document on the Church in the Modern World contains the core of Teilhard's evolution-oriented Christology, which he himself sums up in a simple cry of adoration: "Jesus, the center towards whom all moves." [35] This is the foundation of Teilhard's Christogenesis.

The Christ of Revelation is quite simply Omega. To demonstrate this fundamental proposition, I need only refer to the long series of Johannine and especially Pauline texts where the physical supremacy of Christ over the universe is affirmed in terms which are magnificent . . . They all come to two essential affirmations: 'In eo omnia constant' [in him all things hold together] (Colossians 1:17) and 'Ipse est qui replet omnia' [He it is who fills all things] (Colossians 2:10—cf. Ephesians 4:9), so that 'Omnia in omnibus Christus' [Christ is all, and in all] (Colossians 3:11). There we have the very definition of Omega.[36]

If Christ is Omega, then He is the one single goal and Center of the whole evolutionary process. "The world can no more have two summits than a circumference can have two centers," Teilhard asserts.[37] "A Christic Center for the universe fixed by theology, a cosmic center postulated by anthropogenesis: in the end these two foci necessarily coincide (or at least overlap) in the historical order in which we find ourselves. Christ would not be the sole moving force, the unique outcome for the universe, if the universe in some way, even at a lower level, could gather itself together independently of Him." [38] The universe cannot have two alternative fulfillments any more than the individual man can have two destinies. It is unthinkable because of the essential unity of the universe and of the person. It is the goal, the

34 "Constitution on Church in Modern World," art. 45, Abbott, p. 247.
35 "La Vie Cosmique," *Ecrits*, p. 61.
36 "Mon univers," *Oeuvres* IX, quoted in Mooney, p. 89.
37 *DM*, p. 137. (Translations of Latin are from RSV)
38 "Super-humanité, super-Christ, super-charité," *Oeuvres* IX, pp. 209-10, quoted in Mooney, p. 77.

Omega, that gives meaning and direction to evolution; two dras-
tically different alternative goals such as a "supernatural" and a
"natural" end would be simply unintelligible. The only Omega
that makes cosmogenesis coherent, as we have seen, is a transcendent, pre-existent, autonomous Person. Union with such a
divine Being, the only conceivable end consistent with the nature
of human persons and the direction of cosmogenesis, would necessarily be a transcendent, "supernatural" union beyond the reach
of the created forces of evolution. The fact that this supernatural
end of evolution appears to us as the only wholly satisfying end
does not make it any less gratuitous; it just means that the universe is "graced" right from its "conception" by being destined
for intimate personal union with God—with Christ-Omega
within the inter-personal life of the Trinity, although this is a
goal which the world does not have to attain, theoretically, and,
in fact, cannot attain by its own created power.[39] "What gives
the character of 'gratuity' to the world," Teilhard explains, "is
precisely the fact that the function of universal Center has not
been given to some supreme intermediary between God and the
universe, but has been assumed by God Himself, who in this way
has introduced us into the depths of His immanent Trinitarian
action." [40] "The Kingdom of God is like leaven . . ." Supernatural
grace, the transforming influence of Christ-Omega, penetrates
the universe, suranimates it, without destroying or diminishing
in the least any part of its created autonomy. "The natural and
supernatural fulfillments of the world envelop each other, the
latter incorporating and transforming the former." [41]

The universe, therefore, can have one Center only, at the same time
natural and supernatural, which activates the whole of creation along
one and the same line, towards the greatest possible consciousness,
then towards the highest degree of sanctity, and this Center is Jesus
Christ, personal as well as cosmic.[42]

[39] Cf. Karl Rahner, *Nature and Grace* (New York: Sheed and Ward
1964), pp. 134-141.
[40] "Mon univers," *Oeuvres* IX, p. 84, quoted in Mooney, p. 75.
[41] "Christologie et évolution" (unpubl.), p. 10, quoted in Mooney, p. 206.
Cf. Karl Rahner, S.J., *The Christian Commitment* tr. C. Hastings (New
York: Sheed and Ward, 1963), pp. 53-61, 66-73.
[42] "Forma Christi" (unpubl.), quoted in Mooney, p. 75.

It would be impossible to conceive of a Christ-Omega "who would be organically *central* in the supernatural universe and physically *juxtaposed* in the natural universe," [43] for the simple reason that there are not two universes but one. This single world is a cosmogenesis which by its nature has a supernatural end, and whose evolutionary development is permeated by the supernatural power radiating from that end. For its end is Christ, the Center of its convergence, who draws the world to its gratuitous fulfillment in union with Himself.

Since Christ is Omega, the transcendent Center of universal convergence, and since this converging evolution proceeds by way of "critical points" or "births" towards ever higher being, then the greatest and final "birth," for which the whole of cosmogenesis has been an immense labor, is the birth in space-time of Christ-Omega, who inaugurated by His Incarnation the "last age," the "Christosphere," in which man is lifted up to a totally new super-life and enabled to progress along this super-charged axis towards the final "birth" of the total Christ, the ecstatic union of mankind in Christ-Omega. Cosmogenesis, having progressed through the stage of biogenesis to noogenesis, has been gratuitously suranimated, it has super-evolved into a super-stage of Christogenesis. By the evolutive grace radiating from the now immanent-transcendent Center, the noosphere is transformed, totally transfused with the gratuitous power of Christ, virtually Christified throughout; and yet, historically, noogenesis actually becomes Christogenesis gradually, person by person, or rather, believer by believer, as the grace of Christ is freely received by individuals. This transformation of noogenesis into Christogenesis does not change the direction or manner of evolution; it super-charges it with the grace of Christ. "God unites Himself in such a way to the natural evolution of spirit, taken in its entity, that Christogenesis appears as the sublimation of cosmogenesis." [44] Teilhard summarizes his argument quite simply: "If the world is convergent and if Christ occupies its center,

[43] Letter of January 10, 1920 to Father Auguste Valensin (unpubl.), quoted in Mooney, p. 75.

[44] "Note sur la notion de perfection chrétienne," (unpubl.), p. 2, quoted in Mooney, p. 161.

then the Christogenesis of St. Paul and St. John is nothing else and nothing less than the extension, both awaited and unhoped for, of that noogenesis in which cosmogenesis—as regards our experience—culminates." [45] This is the key to making Christianity relevant to the evolution-conscious men of our day and it is the heart of Teilhard's apologetic. It is demanded, in fact, by the evolutionary character of all our knowledge, whether scientific or theological, and a failure to continuously seek greater penetration into Revelation in the light of our ever increasing human understanding would not only be an infidelity to truth itself, it would also be a partial rejection of Revelation which God has implanted in the collective understanding of man that it might grow and develop with that understanding. Since "we have been forced to abandon the static Aristotelian cosmos and introduced . . . into a universe still in the state of cosmogenesis," Teilhard explains, "we have to rethink our Christology in terms of Christogenesis (at the same time as we rethink our anthropology in terms of anthropogenesis) . . . and from it, I assure you, Christ will emerge in triumph as the saviour of anthropogenesis." [46] The following passage elaborates more fully the value of situating the Mystery of Christ in the context of an evolving world.

By the Incarnation God entered into nature to give it supernatural life and lead it back to Himself: that is the substance of Christian dogma. Of itself this dogma can be accommodated to any number of images in the experimental world. For example, while the human spirit saw in the universe only a fixed arrangement of finished elements, the Christian found no difficulty in situating within this static order the mysterious process of his sanctification. But was this not to some extent a makeshift accommodation? Is a fundamental cosmic immobility really the most favorable setting one could think of for the great spiritual metamorphosis represented by the coming of the Kingdom of God? . . . A universe whose structure evolves—as long as one correctly understands the direction of such a movement— could well be, after all, the milieu most favorable for developing a great and homogeneous understanding of the Incarnation. Christianity found itself stifled by materialistic evolution. But within the large perspectives which are developing of a universe being drawn

[45] *PM*, p. 297.
[46] Letter of April 28, 1954, quoted in Cuénot, p. 362.

upward toward spirit, does it not find a most suitable climate? What better than an ascending anthropogenesis to serve as a background and foundation for the descending illuminations of a Christogenesis? [47]

To probe a little more deeply into the meaning of Christogenesis and to see how Teilhard illumines his ascending anthropogenesis with the Christian Mystery interpreted as a Christogenesis, we must examine first his key theory of Creative Union, and then see the interrelated function he gives to the Incarnation, the Redemption and the Eucharist in the historical progression of Creative Union through Christogenesis towards the Parousia. This time we must start not merely at the beginning, but actually before the beginning of space-time, at the eternal "beginning" when, St. John declares, "the Word was with God, and . . . all things were made through him, and without him was not anything that was made." [48]

Creative Union:
The Trinitarian Source and Goal of Christogenesis

In the beginning was God, the pre-existent, personal Cause of all that is, and in time He revealed Himself as a Divine Trinity. In the awesome inter-personal relations of the triune God, our world was eternally conceived as an apparently and mysteriously "necessary" part of the divine personal activity which Teilhard calls *Trinitization*. God is a divine personal Being. We can conceive of God as opposing and uniting Himself triunely in interpersonal relations; that is, giving of Himself and receiving Himself in an Other, identical in Being and yet Other, and expressing this mutual relationship, eternally and infinitely, by a joint giving and receiving with a third Equal yet Other than them both. This is the twofold movement, the interpersonal giving and receiving that is the essence of Trinitization. [49] Within it our world as-

[47] "La Mystique de la Science," *Oeuvres* VI, pp. 220-21, quoted in Mooney, p. 69.
[48] John 1:1, 3 (RSV).
[49] "Comment je vois" (unpubl.), p. 17 and note 26, quoted in Mooney, p. 171. On Creative Union and Trinitization, cf. Mooney, pp. 169-177.

sumes the completing function of an extrinsic *Other* in which the
three divine Persons may jointly express their triune relations and
their unity. For Trinitization causes a certain divine "necessity"
to arise within the Trinity to express or extend their communal
act outside themselves, by opposing to themselves in unity an
infinite multiplicity (ultimately a multiplicity of persons), and
then, by a united self-giving to the created *others* outside themselves, to draw them to perfect unity, even in the "super-
intimacy" of their own trinitarian union—"that they may all be
one; even as thou, Father, art in me, and I in thee, that they also
may be one in us . . ." [50] This created reflection of Trinitization
Teilhard calls *Pleromization*, which he defines as "the giving of
reality to participated being through arrangement and totalization." [51] The Pleroma, then, is the totalized (completed in unity)
world of participated beings drawn into personal union within
the Trinity. In other words, since it is a "replica or symmetry of
Trinitization, Pleromization means the creative process by which
the Triune First Cause unites personally to Himself the "creatible
void" of "pure multiplicity" (nothingness) that is at the "antipodes of His absolute Oneness." [52] Since "to create is to unite,"
and to unite to a very precise personal End, then to create is to
elicit a directed process of unification, a cosmogenesis. Creation is
a continuous process whose expression is the converging evolution of the world and whose term is the fullness of the Pleroma.[53] And "the mysterious Pleroma" which is the end of Creative Union is a Fullness "in which the substantial *One* and the
created *many* fuse without confusion in a *whole* which, without
adding anything essential to God will nevertheless be a sort of
triumph and generalization of being," Teilhard writes.[54]

"What is the active center, the living link, the organizing soul
of the Pleroma?" Teilhard asks. How, in other words, does the

[50] John 17:21.
[51] "Comment je vois," (unpubl.), pp. 18-19, quoted in Mooney, pp. 172-173.
[52] *Ibid.*
[53] Cf. R. Faricy, S.J., *Teilhard de Chardin's Theology of the Christian & the World* (New York: Sheed & Ward, 1967), ch. 4.
[54] *DM*, p. 100.

Trinity effect this personal unification of all created reality in union with Itself? Teilhard answers: "St. Paul, again, proclaims it with all his resounding voice: it is He in whom everything is reunited, and in whom all things are consummated—through whom the whole created edifice receives its consistence—Christ dead and risen *who fills all, in whom all things hold together*." [55] We are including here the rich passages from St. Paul so that we can see at once how these were the source of Teilhard's idea of the function of the Cosmic Christ in Pleromization.

Therein lies the richness of God's free grace lavished upon us, imparting full wisdom and insight. He has made known to us His hidden purpose—such was His will and pleasure determined beforehand in Christ—to be put into effect when the time was ripe: namely, that the universe, all in heaven and on earth, might be brought into a unity in Christ.[56]

For we are God's handiwork, created in Christ Jesus . . .[57]

He is the image of the invisible God; his is the primacy over all created things. In him everything in heaven and on earth was created . . . : the whole universe has been created through him and for him. And he exists before everything and all things are held together in him . . . Through him God chose to reconcile the whole universe to himself . . . through him alone.[58]

Teilhard can do no more than develop in the light of his converging cosmogenesis these magnificent lines of St. Paul. "I find it quite impossible," he writes, "to read St. Paul without being dazzled by the vision under his words of the universal and cosmic dominance of the Incarnate Word." [59] Christ is He "in whom everything is created and He in whom the entire world in all its depth, its length, its breadth, its grandeur, its physical and its spiritual, comes to be and takes on consistency . . . The world is above all a work of continuous creation in Christ," Teilhard concludes, paraphrasing St. Paul. Therefore, the Pleroma, which is

[55] *DM*, pp. 100-101.
[56] Eph. 1:8-10. (New English Bible).
[57] Eph. 2:10 (NEB).
[58] Col. 1:15-20 (NEB).
[59] "Mon univers," *Oeuvres* IX (n.p.), quoted in de Lubac, *T. de C. the Man* . . ., p. 35.

defined by the Scripture exegetes as "the universe filled with the creative presence of God," [60] or, in Teilhard's terms, the universe filled with the unitive presence of Omega—this Pleroma is summed up in Christ who is its principle, its center of cohesion and harmony.[61] "The mysterious synthesis of the Uncreated and the created, the great fulfillment—both quantitative and qualitative—of the Universe in God," which is Teilhard's description of the Pleroma, "finds its physical principle, its expression and its stability in the figure of Christ-Omega, the Universal Christ." [62] It was conceived in Him and is continuously being created in Him because He is its end and fulfillment, the Image in whom nothingness took on form.[63]

In Christ the eternal Word, the Father, as principle of the eternal processions within the Trinity, opposes and unites Himself; and in Him, therefore, He conceives of the infinite multiplicity, the "creatible void," which He feels constrained, as it were, by His love, to oppose to Himself as a created extension of the Word, and to draw into a union with Himself by an extension of that same act by which He unites the Word to Himself in the Spirit. The evolving universe, therefore, which the Father creates in and through the Son by the Spirit exists and is becoming one in the Son, the Word. The creative process itself, Pleromization, by which the universe is drawn into the Son, reflects "Trinitization" not only because its existence and fulfillment consists in being opposed and united with the Trinity, but because the act of opposing and uniting is done in a unique manner, although conjointly, by each of the three divine Persons, and thus expresses, as well as their unity, their inner personal distinction. "Participated being," therefore, is most basically (and the more so the more it is personal) participated relationship, and

[60] P. Benoit, quoted in F. X. Durrwell, *The Resurrection*, trans. R. Sheed (New York: Sheed and Ward, 1960), p. 116.

[61] Durrwell, pp. 106, 115-118, Cf. Lucien Cerfaux, *Christ in the Theology of St. Paul* (New York: Herder, 1959), pp. 172, 242, 401, 426-9.

[62] "La parole attendue," *Cahiers Pierre de Chardin*, IV (Paris: Seuil, 1963), pp. 26-27.

[63] Cf. Jean Mouroux, *The Mystery of Time*, trans. J. Drury (New York: Desclee, 1962), p. 88.

precisely participated Sonship; yet this indicates a "supernatural" fulfillment of participated being which requires a further gratuitous step in the creative process, a step, however, *in view of which* the process was begun, that is, the Incarnation. By the grace of the Incarnate Word, the cosmos will be consummated in personal union with the Son, as His Pleroma, and will be incorporated into the Son's eternal relations with the Father and the Spirit. This is Christ's revelation in His prayer to the Father: "that they may be one even as we are one, *I in them and thou in me,* that they may become perfectly one, so that the world may know that thou hast sent me, and hast *loved them even as thou hast loved me.*" [64] It is for the consummation of this union that Christ tells us, "The Father is working still and I am working." [65] And it will be the personal union in vision for which mankind yearns with the full force of cosmogenesis that will mark this completion of the Pleroma, a vision foreshadowed even now, in this last age of the Spirit by Christian faith: "In that day you will know that I am in my Father, and you in me, and I in you . . . These things I have spoken to you, that my joy may be in you and that your joy may be full." [66] But we are anticipating a point in Teilhard's synthesis which we have yet to develop.

The Incarnation:
The Universe as Christ's Body-in-Evolution

The Incarnation is the focal point of Creative Union, the essential act through which God achieves Pleromization. The Word in whom the Father unites the universe to Himself is not the pre-existent Word as such but the Incarnate Word. Although Christ is the pre-existent Omega "from whom are all things and to whom are all things," it is somehow only in virtue of His Incarnation, involving His Death and Resurrection, that He has been the principle and keystone of the cosmos right from the begin-

[64] John 17:22-23 (RSV) (emphasis added).
[65] John 5:17.
[66] John 14:20; 15:11.

ning. Only by immersing Himself in the universe could He seize
hold of the axial force of evolution, as it were, and super-charge
it with the dynamism of His own Holy Spirit.[67] If the Risen
Lord is the Omega of cosmogenesis and the Cause of Pleromization, then the process of Creative Union began, as we have already indicated, with the redemptive Incarnation of the Son in
view. "The prodigious extent of time before the first Christmas,"
therefore, Teilhard writes, "was not void of Him but penetrated
throughout by His powerful influence." [68] God "willed His
Christ, and in order to have His Christ He had to create a world
of the spirit, men in particular, in which Christ would germinate;
and to have man, He had to launch the enormous movement of
organic life . . . ; and for the latter to spring up the whole tumult
of the cosmos was necessary." [69] We may say, then, that creation
was for the sake of the redemptive Incarnation, since it was for
the sake of the Pleroma which is essentially the completion of the
Incarnation, or the fullness of the Incarnate Word. The "necessity" of the Incarnation, however, is the necessity of divine love,
which is at once an absolute freedom, and in no way denies the
gratuity of the Incarnation, even though it points out that creation and "elevation" are inseparable in the divine intention, as far
as we can judge. It simply means that, in the words of a noted
theologian, "the world's being is this: to be destined for Christ
from time immemorial, and creation is impregnated with Christ
as its foundation and goal." [70] Teilhard explains the role and
"necessity" of the Incarnation in the following summary from
The Phenomenon of Man:

As early as St. Paul and St. John we read that to create, to fulfill and
to purify the world is, for God, to unify it by uniting it organically
with himself. How does he unify it? By partially immersing himself in
things, by becoming 'element,' and then, from this point of vantage in
the heart of matter, assuming the control and leadership of what we
now call evolution. Christ, principle of universal vitality because

[67] Cf. Durrwell, pp. 115-116.
[68] "Mon univers," *Oeuvres* IX, p. 89, quoted in Mooney, p. 168.
[69] *Ibid.,* pp. 169-170.
[70] Heinrich Schlier, "The Domination of Christ," *The Christian and the
World* (New York: P. J. Kenedy and Sons, 1965), p. 104.

sprung up as man among men, put himself in the position (maintained ever since) to subdue under himself, to purify, to direct and superanimate the general ascent of consciousness into which he inserted himself. By a perennial act of communion and sublimation, he aggregates to himself the total psychism of the earth. And when he has gathered everything together and transformed everything, he will close in upon himself and his conquests, thereby rejoining, in a final gesture, the divine focus he has never left . . . God *shall be all in all.*[71]

By His Incarnation, therefore, Christ becomes the organic or physical Center of the universe in the sense that the universe even on the natural level is dependent on Him for its fulfillment and for the energies by which it progresses toward that fulfillment. "All energies hold together, are welded deep down into a single whole, and what the humanity of Our Lord does is to take them up again and reweld them in a transcendent and personal unity." [72] The redemptive Incarnation has so completely recast the world that actually "there is only one dynamism: that which leads everything to Jesus," so that the world will only "reach completion on the natural level by reason of its relationship to Him." [73] As the ultimate psychic Center for the gathering together of the whole universe, Christ the Incarnate Word superanimates the whole cosmos, penetrating it with the influence of His personal attraction, progressively uniting man so totally to Himself in love and at the same time subjecting the whole universe in man to Himself that it becomes the perfect expression and revelation of His own personal Being, which is the same as saying until it becomes His totalized cosmic Body. "By His Incarnation," Teilhard explains, "He inserted Himself not just into humanity but into the universe which supports humanity, and He did so not simply as another connected element, but with the dignity and function of a directing principle, of a Center towards which everything converges in harmony and in love," [74] that is, as the directing principle of a Person personalizing His own

[71] *PM*, pp. 293-294.

[72] Letter of February 2, 1916, *MM*, p. 93.

[73] Letter of December 12, 1919, in *Archives de Philosophie*, xxiv (1961), pp. 139-40, quoted in Mooney, p. 75.

[74] "La Vie cosmique," *Ecrits*, pp. 39-40, quoted in Mooney, p. 70.

Body. "All things insofar as they converge toward Christ, under His attraction, to be fulfilled in Him in the Pleroma," constitute this "cosmic Body of Christ." [75] The identification of the Pleroma with the Body of Christ is to be understood not in any analogous sense, Teilhard insists, but "boldly, as it was seen by St. John, St. Paul and the Fathers": as "an organism moving and alive in which we are all united physically." [76] And recognizing the universe-in-evolution as Christ's Body-in-evolution, which is the necessary conclusion of the theory of Creative Union, "is nothing but the development of what the Church teaches us concerning the growth of Christ." It is the philosophy of the universe conceived in function of our knowledge of the Mystical Body." It simply means that, in the community of Christians summing up in themselves the whole universe, "the world is still being created and it is Christ who is bringing Himself to completion in it." [77] Also, considering the world as the Body of Christ is simply applying to Him, in the limitless extent demanded by His function as Omega, the relationship which every human person has to the cosmos. For the matter of the body which a person's soul informs cannot be limited to "what is covered by skin," but, in a way that is unique with each one and quite limited, it extends to the whole universe.[78] "The consciousness which we are gradually acquiring of our physical relationship with all parts of the Universe represents a genuine enlarging of our separate personalities . . . In the domain external to our flesh our *real and whole body* is continuing to take shape." [79] This point is very important for understanding the realism of the Body of Christ concept. Teilhard describes this cosmic extension of the human body as an aura:

There is nothing strange about there being a universal physical element in Christ. Each one of us, if we but reflect, is enveloped, aureoled, by an extension of his being as vast as the universe. What we are aware of is only the nucleus which is ourselves. But the

[75] "L'element universal," *Ecrits*, pp. 405-408.

[76] "La Vie Cosmique," *Ecrits*, pp. 39-40, quoted in Mooney, p. 70.

[77] "L'union créatrice," 15, quoted in Mooney, p. 170.

[78] Karl Rahner, *Theology of Death*, p. 30. Cf. also: Leo Scheffczyk, "The Meaning of Christ's Parousia," *The Christian and the World*, pp. 141-142.

[79] "A Note on Progress," *FM*, p. 17.

interaction of monads would be incomprehensible if an "aura" did not extend from one to the other, that is, something proper to each one and common to all. How then are we to imagine the constitution of Christ as cosmic Center of creation? Simply as an extension, a transformation, brought about in the Humanity of Jesus, of that "aura" which surrounds every human nomad.[80]

This understanding of the relationship of the individual to the cosmos by an extension of his body explains how Christ could become "co-extensive with the physical immensities of duration and space without losing the preciseness of his humanity." [81] The Christ who is "invested with the power to give the World, in him, its *definitive form*," and who "has been consecrated for a cosmic function," is the historical Jesus. "Men are called to form a single body . . . and the Humanity of Jesus has been *chosen* to serve as the instrument for this unification in which the scattered cluster of all the fibres that make up the Universe is closely knit.[82] Teilhard insists on the identity of the historical and cosmic Christ, for the only way that the Word could unite to Himself the entire created universe, as we know it, would be to enter into it as *a* Man, and then by extending Himself beyond the limitations of His historical body to incorporate into Himself the whole of Man, that is, the community of Mankind with their cosmic body. Moreover,

if you suppress the historical reality of Christ, the divine omni-presence which intoxicates us becomes, like all the other dreams of metaphysics, uncertain, vague, conventional—lacking the decisive experimental verification by which to impose itself on our minds, and without the moral directives to assimilate our lives into it. Thenceforward, however dazzling the expansions which we shall try in a moment to discern in the resurrected Christ, their beauty and their stuff of reality will always remain inseparable from the tangible and verifiable truth of the Gospel event. The mystical Christ, the universal

[80] "Forma Christi," *Ecrits*, p. 239, quoted in Mooney, p. 79. Cf. *DM*, pp. 122-125.

[81] "Esquisse d'un univers personnel," *Oeuvres* VI, p. 113, quoted in Mooney, pp. 80-81.

[82] "Forma Christi," *Ecrits*, p. 335, quoted in de Lubac, *T. de C. the Man* . . ., p. 31.

Christ of St. Paul, has neither meaning nor value in our eyes except as an expansion of the Christ who was born of Mary and who died on the Cross. The former essentially draws His fundamental quality of undeniability and concreteness from the latter. However we may be drawn into the divine spaces opened up to us by Christian mysticism, we never depart from the Jesus of the Gospels.[83]

The Redemptive Death and Resurrection: Christogenesis Spirit-charged and Guaranteed Fulfillment

Thus, "the universe takes on the lineaments of Jesus; but then there is great mystery: for he who thus becomes discernable is Jesus crucified."[84] The Incarnation is by its very nature redemptive, because it means that the Word, Omega, has "emptied Himself" by entering into and taking hold of the world-in-evolution at a stage of sin-heightened disorganization or disunity when it was not yet ready to be fully united to Himself. In fact, having immersed Himself in this world as a single isolated individual man at a rather primitive stage in noogenesis, Christ assumed the whole condition of such a man at such a stage of universal disunity in the physical and moral orders. "He was made sin for us,"[85] in the sense that He assumed all the evil inherent in the world. Teilhard describes the Incarnation, therefore, as a "kenosis into matter."[86] He further explains:

In the context of convergent cosmogenesis, to create is, for God, to unite: and to unite with something is to become immersed in it. But to be immersed (in Plurality) is to 'corpusculize' oneself: and this, in a world whose organization statistically entails disorder (and, mechanically, effort) means plunging (in order to overcome them) into imperfection and pain . . . God cannot appear as Prime Mover towards the future without becoming Incarnate and without redeeming, that is without *Christifying Himself* for us.[87]

83 *DM*, pp. 94-95.
84 "Le Prêtre," *Ecrits*, pp. 285-302, quoted in *HU*, p. 153.
85 2 Cor. 5:21, (RSV).
86 "Mon univers," *Oeuvres* IX, p. 90.
87 "From Cosmos to Cosmogenesis," *Oeuvres* VII, pp. 261-277, quoted in Cuénot, p. 292.

Evil appears in Teilhard's system as a necessary and unavoidable part of a converging cosmogenesis. To progress from disunity to unity in a universe whose evolution is marked by two uncertainties, "chance at the bottom and . . . freedom at the top," inevitably involves an ordering of a disordered multiplicity that is experienced by man physically and psychologically as painful—the pain of growth, or of suffering and death, or of solitude and anxiety; and it also involves, by statistical necessity, that some elements are left behind in the process of "arrangement and centration," either lost to entropy by the play of chance, or, on the human level, lost to "some mysterious antipodes of spirit," some "infinite splintering of consciousness upon itself," which is the damnation that men may bring on themselves who, by a perverse use of their freedom, reject the whole process of unification and union in Omega.[88] "It is necessary that scandals happen," Our Lord says, and these words run like a refrain through Teilhard's explanations of the place of evil in a converging universe.[89] A universe, in other words, created out of a Nothingness conceived of as pure multiplicity, in a process of progressive unification, necessarily involves the evil of failure, disorganization, and painful growth or synthesis all along the way, but it is an evil that, in all its forms, is but the reverse side of an immense triumph.[90]

It follows from our analysis that it is *not at all out of powerlessness* but on account *of the very structure of Nothingness* over which he bends in order to create, God can only proceed in one way: arranging, unifying little by little, under the attraction of his influence, by using the groping interplay of great numbers . . . The unavoidable counterpart of any success obtained in this way is that it has to be paid for by a certain proportion of waste products. Disharmony or physical decomposition in the preliving domain, pain among the living, sin in the domain of freedom. There is no *order in the process of formation* which, at all degrees, does not imply some disorder . . . If (as we must, I believe, necessarily admit) there is for our understand-

[88] "Introduction à la vie chrétienne," (unpubl.), p. 9, quoted in Mooney, p. 131; "Forma Christi," 1918, in *Ecrits*, pp. 349-5, quoted in Mooney, p. 129; *PM*, pp. 310-311.
[89] Eg. *PM*, p. 310; *DM*, p. 58.
[90] "The New Spirit, 1942," *FM*, p. 90.

ing only one possible way in which God can create—that is, through evolution, by way of unification—Evil is an unavoidable by-product; it looks like a shadow which cannot be separated from Creation.[91]

Human toil and suffering in such a world in evolution toward unity are the necessary price of final human victory. "The world, looked at empirically on our scale, is an immense groping, an immense search, an immense attack; it can only progress at the cost of many failures and many casualties." [92]

Sin, the basic evil of the world, becomes reflective and free in man, who seems to emerge with an increasing "constitutional urge to exist proudly and selfishly." [93] Matter appears to offer a resistance against which the forward movement of evolution (complexity/consciousness, radial energy) must constantly struggle to achieve ever increasing arrangement and centration or synthesis. On the human level this resistance becomes a conscious and free, therefore morally culpable, rejection of noogenesis, in its ascent towards unification by ever increasing love of Omega. With the fullness of Christian revelation, this "sin of the world" culminates in the deliberate rejection of Christ which separates individual men from the only source of love, and hence, of fulfillment in unification.[94] The great evil, therefore, is the sinful refusal to love Christ and a consequent limitation of the love energy necessary for evolution, and it is an evil which, theoretically, could triumph and cause the final regression of the universe into the nothingness of multiplicity from which it was drawn.[95]

Christ, by His Redemptive Incarnation, has overcome this sin of the world, however, and for a Christian believer the final success of cosmogenesis in man "is positively guaranteed by the 'redeeming virtue' of the God incarnate in his creation." [96] "The

[91] "Comment je vois," (unpubl.), p. 30, quoted in Piet Schoonenberg, *Man and Sin,* (Notre Dame: Notre Dame Press, 1965), p. 44.

[92] "The Meaning and Constructive Value of Suffering," (tr. N. Lindsay), in Neville Braybrooke, *Teilhard de Chardin, Pilgrim of the Future* (New York: Seabury, 1964), p. 25.

[93] Letter of January 1, 1917, *MM*, p. 160.

[94] Schoonenberg, *Man and Sin,* pp. 107, 118-23.

[95] "Le Phénomène Spirituel," 1937, *Oeuvres*, VI, p. 134 and note 2.

[96] *PM*, p. 307, footnote 1.

eventual biological success of Man on Earth is not merely a probability but a certainty [born of a supernatural act of faith]: since Christ (and in Him virtually the World) is already risen." [97] Christ, dead and risen, becomes "the principle of unity that saves a guilty creation from returning to dust . . . Jesus comes to reestablish at the heart of the world the harmony of efforts and the convergence of all things . . . [by] the unification of all flesh in one same Spirit." [98] It is Christ's death which achieves the triumph of the Resurrection and the release into the heart of the world of the Spirit of love. Death "is evil itself" and Christ's death is the ultimate point of His "kenosis into matter," and "the complete immersion of the Divine Unity in the ultimate depths of multiplicity." [99] But death is also the highest possible act of human love; it is the final act by which the human person becomes himself.[100] Christ's death is the culminating act of His Incarnate, redemptive Being, a Spirit-informed love-act by which He breaks down the isolating barriers of His own body of flesh and rises with His glorified cosmic Body,[101] thus becoming Himself, the Son of God established in power. "For isn't it death, in fact, that liberates, that breaks down the barriers that keep the soul in isolation and allows it to lose itself in God?" [102] When He handed Himself over to the Father in the act of death, Jesus, summing up in Himself the totality of humanity and hence the whole cosmos, said a definitive *yes* to the Father's plan of Pleromization and became the dynamic Spirit-communicating Center of universal convergence. It is at His Death-Resurrection that the Incarnate Word assumes His place as Omega, at once at the apex and at the axial center of cosmogenesis "whence His Spirit can radiate through all the centuries and all beings." [103]

[97] "The Directions and Conditions of the Future," *FM*, p. 237.
[98] "La Lutte contra la Multitude," *Ecrits*, p. 124.
[99] "Mon univers," *Oeuvres* IX, p. 89.
[100] Ladislaus Boros, S.J., *The Mystery of Death* (New York: Herder, 1965), pp. 42-7.
[101] Cf. Durrwell, p. 186: "We may say that the body of Christ rose as a Mystical Body."
[102] Letter of January 16, 1917, *MM*, p. 164.
[103] "The New Spirit, 1942," *FM*, p. 94.

Omega Himself saves the world by immersing Himself in it, super-charging its evolutionary drive with the power of His Spirit, and, by progressively assimilating it to Himself as His Body, leads it to fulfillment in Himself. Thus, "the suffering Christ, without ever ceasing to be He who carries the sins of the world, and precisely *as such*, is . . . He who carries and supports the weight of the world in its process of evolution." [104] "In other words, Christ the Redeemer, without in the least losing the marks of His Passion, [is] seen in the fullness of His power as Christ the Evolver." [105] By the love-act of surrender to the Father that was the essence of His death, Jesus broke down within Himself and for all men the isolation inherent in the human condition and the root of man's selfishness and perverted autonomy. Christ's "Into thy hands" is the cry of adoration that breathes for the Spirit of the new creation; and it is the Spirit who super-charges man's love energy, the axial power of noogenesis, with divine agape, transforming noogenesis into Christogenesis—again, believer by believer. The very sufferings entailed in His Passion became for Christ the necessary battle for the triumph of the human spirit over its materialistic egoism, the victory over the resistance to spiritual ascent that is inherent in matter.[106] He, and in Him all mankind, "learned obedience"—and love and adoration, the ultimate force of evolution—"through the things which he suffered." [107] Christ's sufferings and death, because born in tremendous love, are redemptive because they mark a dynamic and definitive ascent which was, by that very fact, a reparation for the sin that was a descent back into multiplicity. "The Incarnate Word's work of salvation," therefore, is *"primario* to lead creation to its fulfillment in union with the divine, and for this purpose *secundario* [and as a consequence] to eliminate the evil forces of regression and dispersion." [108]

In the light of Christ's Death-Resurrection, the toil and suffer-

---

[104] "Introduction à la vie chrétienne" (unpubl.), p. 8.
[105] "Le Christ évoluteur" (unpubl.), pp. 6-7, quoted in Mooney, p. 106.
[106] "Christologie et évolution" (unpubl.), p. 8.
[107] Heb. 5:8.
[108] "Le Christ évoluteur," 1942, pp. 6-7.

ing and death that form the substance of human life take on tremendous value. The Cross of Christ becomes the symbol of the "way of universal progress." [109] It teaches that "life has a term; therefore it imposes a particular direction, oriented, in fact, towards the greatest possible spiritualization by means of the greatest possible effort." [110] "The royal road of the Cross is no more nor less than the road of human endeavour supernaturally righted and prolonged." [111] Summarizing his thought, Teilhard writes:

Jesus on the Cross is both the symbol and the reality of the immense labor of the centuries which has, little by little, raised up the created spirit and brought it back to the depths of the divine context. He represents (and in a true sense, He is) creation, as, sustained by God, it reascends the slopes of being, sometimes clinging to things for support, sometimes tearing itself from them in order to transcend them, and always compensating, by physical suffering, for the setbacks caused by its moral downfalls.[112]

Therefore, "once we have fully grasped the meaning of the Cross, we are no longer in danger of finding life sad and ugly. We shall simply have become more attentive to its incomprehensible gravity." [113] In saving the world, Christ could not free us from suffering and death, nor even from moral failure, since these are a necessary and inseparable part of the evolutionary process itself; but He could, and did, transform them into the most powerful instruments of the world's transformation. "Like an artist making use of the fault or an impurity in the stone he is sculpting or the bronze he is casting to produce more exquisite lines or a more beautiful tone, God, without sparing us the partial deaths, nor the final death, which form an essential part of our lives, transfigures them . . . *provided we trust lovingly in Him* . . . by making them serve our conscious fulfillment." [114] Suffering, and ultimately death, are the active "agents" of our spiritualization;

[109] *DM*, p. 78.
[110] *DM*, p. 77.
[111] *DM*, p. 78.
[112] *DM*, p. 79.
[113] *DM*, pp. 78-9.
[114] *DM*, p. 58.

they enable us progressively, then finally and totally, to lose our foothold on this earth, and even "within ourselves," and to go out of ourselves in an ecstasy of loving surrender to God. Sufferings of all sorts are "the very real forms of that ecstasy which is to tear us from ourselves so as to subordinate us to God." [115] But we must cross this "critical point of our ex-centration" and allow God to penetrate into our inmost selves in order to achieve that absolute Center-to-center union with Him in which the whole of our world will be divinized; for "union with Christ presupposes essentially that we transpose the center of our existence into Him—which implies the radical sacrifice of our egoism," fully attainable only in death.[116] For our completion as well as the whole world's "is only consummated through a death, a 'night', a reversal, an ex-centration, and a quasi-depersonalization," [117] which is, in fact, the super-personalization, individual and communal, that marks the fullness of union in the Pleroma.

By conquering death Christ has brought the essential hope and the *joie de vivre* without which man's efforts to conquer the earth would inevitably falter and come to a halt. Thus, an "irreplaceable role of Christianity," Teilhard asserts, is this marvelous transformation of suffering into a sublime expression of love and therefore an activity of prime importance for the progress of noogenesis. This doesn't mean that the Christian is to submit passively to suffering; he must struggle energetically against the evil inherent in every type of pain, and only at the optimum of his resistance can a loving surrender to God be the flower of fidelity to His will.

Suffering is still to be treated at first as an adversary and fought against right to the end; yet at the same time we must accept it insofar as it can uproot our egoism and center us more completely on God. Yes, dark and repulsive though it is, suffering has been revealed to us as a supremely active principle for the humanization and the divinization of the universe. Here is the ultimate meaning for that

[115] *DM*, p. 60.
[116] *DM*, p. 66.
[117] Letter of December 12, 1919 to Auguste Valensin, in *Pierre Teilhard de Chardin, Maurice Blondell: Correspondence* (New York: Herder & Herder, 1967), p. 31, (hereafter cited as *Correspondence*).

prodigious spiritual energy born of the Cross . . . A growth of spirit arising from the deficiency of matter. A possible Christification of suffering. This is indeed the miracle which has been constantly renewed for the past two thousand years.[118]

Such a realization, while not diminishing the pain of those who are suffering, can buoy them up with new courage and a sense of dignity in the most humbling of trials. It reassures them that "they are not useless and diminished elements" without value in the world's ascent, but rather are "those who pay the price of universal progress and triumph. They are the ones who have fallen on the field of honor." It is especially the sick and the suffering who "find themselves as it were driven out of themselves" as they "bear in their enfeebled bodies the weight of the moving world, who find themselves, by the just disposition of providence, the most active factor in that very process which seems to sacrifice and shatter them." They are the ones *chosen* "to give breath to their brothers who labor like miners in the depths of matter." [119] The key to the transformation of suffering is love, a personal love of Christ, that prompts us to unite with Him in the "fellowship of His sufferings," and He alone is the source of this love. To suffer and die redemptively in Christ, our suffering and death must be "informed" or empowered, as His was, by the Holy Spirit. To plumb the depths of the mystery of suffering, therefore, brings us into the heart of Christian mysticism, which we shall take up in the last chapter.

The Eucharist and the Eucharistic Community:
The Physical, Operative Center of Christogenesis

We have attempted to trace the main lines of Teilhard's evolution-oriented Christology, showing that Creation, Incarnation, and Redemption are the essentially interrelated divine acts that make up the all-embracing mystery of Creative Union. They are

[118] "L'Énergie spirituelle de la souffrance," *Oeuvres* VII, pp. 256-7, quoted in Mooney, p. 114.
[119] "The Meaning and Constructive Value of Suffering," in Braybrooke, p. 25.

the steps in Pleromization through which cosmogenesis becomes Christogenesis. "Creation, Incarnation and Redemption, each mark a higher degree of gratuity of the divine operation, but are they not also three acts which are indissolubly united in the appearance of participated being?" [120]

Thus it is that a series of ideas, long regarded as independent, come gradually more and more to link themselves together organically before our eyes. Up to a certain point there is no God (that is, considered in His *Pleroma*) without creative union, no creation without (God's) incarnate immersion into it, no Incarnation without redemptive compensation . . . The three fundamental 'mysteries' of Christianity are seen to be but three aspects of a single mystery of mysteries, that of Pleromization, or the reduction of multiplicity to unity.[121]

Even more concisely and clearly, Teilhard shows the interrelatedness of these three aspects of Pleromization by stating that there is just "one single process, which is Christogenesis, considered either in its moving principle (creation), or in its unifying mechanism (Incarnation), or in its uplifted struggle (Redemption)." [122] It remains now for us to examine briefly how, in Teilhard's system, this threefold process continues pleromizing the universe until its culmination at the Parousia. The great means by which Christ incorporates mankind and the universe into Himself is the Eucharist, which operates most intensively in the Church which it creates.

Through the Eucharist Christ manifests His active, unifying presence radiating outward, super-animating and assimilating the world into Himself. The Eucharist operates as "the expression and manifestation of the divine unifying energy applying itself little by little to every spiritual atom of the universe." [123] By means of the Eucharist Christ draws the believer to Himself in an intimate Spirit-communicating embrace, for the Eucharist contact with Christ is the point of "maximum penetration and activation." [124] Through the Eucharist there "passes directly the axis of

120 "L'Ame du monde," *Ecrits*, p. 231, quoted in Mooney, p. 177.
121 "Comment je vois" (unpubl.), pp. 20-21, quoted in Mooney, pp. 176-77.
122 "Introduction à la vie chrétienne," 3, quoted in Mooney, p. 177.
123 *Ibid.*, p. 86.
124 "Le Christique" (unpubl.), p. 8, quoted in Mooney, pp. 86-87.

the Incarnation, that is to say the axis of creation." We touch and
enter into the very heart of Christogenesis, the dynamic Center
of the Christosphere, and line up the whole of our activity with
the axial drive of a divinized universe-in-ascent, in every Eucharistic celebration. "To unite ourselves to Christ in the Eucharist,
therefore, is *ipso facto* inevitably to incorporate ourselves little
by little into a Christogenesis which is in itself the soul of
cosmogenesis." [125]

The immediate effect of this intensely dynamic contact with
Christ of all who believe in Him is the communion of believers,
stretching from the beginning to the end of mankind's history, in
one great communion. And all who are united in this communion
of the Eucharistic Body form around Christ-Omega, the Center
of universal convergence, the nucleus of the unanimization of
mankind that is the condition of the Parousia. From this inner
core (or phylum) of Spirit-empowered Christians Christ can expand outwards to finally draw into communion with Himself the
total Body of Mankind. Thus, "it is around Christianity (considered in its 'phyletic' or Catholic form) that the principal axis of
hominization coils itself ever tighter." [126] The transforming action of Christ radiates outward from His Eucharistic Body,
which is identified by extension with His Church, into the whole
universe. The consuming of the consecrated Bread and Wine
representing the world progressing through our labor and our
suffering is a symbol or, rather, a Sacrament which effects
Christ's assimilation, through His Eucharistic Community, the
Church, of the entire cosmos into Himself.

As our humanity assimilates the material world, and as the Host
assimilates our humanity, the eucharistic transformation goes beyond
and completes the transubstantiation of the bread on the altar. Step
by step it irresistibly invades the universe. It is the fire that sweeps
over the heath; the stroke that vibrates through the bronze. In a
secondary and generalized sense, the sacramental Species are formed
by the totality of the world, and the duration of creation is the time
needed for its consecration.[127]

[125] "Introduction à la vie chrétienne," p. 10, quoted in Mooney, p. 86.
[126] "Christianisme et évolution" (unpubl.), p. 10, quoted in Mooney, p. 159.
[127] *DM*, p. 104.

The Eucharist, therefore, is the essential "instrument" of Pleromization, and the very act of pleromization is identifiable with the act of transubstantiation, which is "not limited to the material particle that [Christ's] brief presence volatilizes," but "is aureoled with a real divinization of the whole universe. From the cosmic element into which He inserts Himself, the Word acts to subjugate all else and assimilate it to Himself." [128]

It is by our active labor in every conceivable field as well as by our suffering that, continually purified and energized by our Eucharistic contact with Christ, we "assimilate the material world" so that it might become in us Christ's Body. The power of the Eucharist extends outward through the activity and the personal relationships of the members of the Eucharistic Community primarily, although it works also through those who labor honestly outside the intimacy of that communion. The universal extent of Eucharistic transubstantiation, therefore, depends actually on the cooperation of Christians working and suffering in the world, a point that we shall consider in its implications for the spiritual life in the next section.

The Parousia:
Christogenesis Fulfilled—The Revelation of the Cosmic Christ

When will the Pleroma be completed and the universe at last drawn into the perfect unity of the Body of Christ? "What will be the signs of your coming . . . ? . . . Of that day and hour no one knows, not even the Son." [129] Without presuming to predict the "day and hour," Teilhard proposes the conditions which he feels we should rationally expect to see fulfilled before Christ can manifest Himself in the glory of His pleromized Body. Following the laws of complexity/consciousness, Christified to the core in the sphere of Christogenesis (without in any way destroying, but rather perfecting, the natural operation of its progress), the world must have reached its final critical point of planetary

---

[128] "Le Prêtre," *Ecrits*, p. 287, quoted in Mooney, p. 82.
[129] Matt. 24:3, 36.

maturation before Christ can appropriately reveal Himself in it, for the natural progress of cosmic evolution is inseparably bound up with the "supernatural" readiness of the world for the final vision of Him in the glory of His Pleroma. The world must reach an "excess of unification and co-reflection" before it can experience, at this "critical point," its final rebirth into Christ-Omega.[130] This critical point will coincide with the convergence at their common pole of three simultaneous and interrelated lines of progress: 1) the total assimilation of the material universe into the human synthesis of co-reflection, which will have been effected by man's research and invention, motivated, in turn, and suranimated by a common passion to build the New Earth, the Body of Christ; 2) the unanimization of mankind in the bond of the Spirit effected ultimately by the Eucharist; and finally, 3) the mystical union of mankind with Christ, expressed in an ecstatic *maranatha* cry for total union through a final death. The natural consummation of cosmogenesis is a condition, therefore, although not a cause, of the Parousia; and so, to hasten Christ's coming we must labor to form that noospheric Brain and Heart which alone can become the "eyes and heart" that "see God." Teilhard argues:

We continue from force of habit to think of the Parousia . . . as an event of a purely catastrophic nature—that is to say, liable to come about at any moment in history, irrespective of any definite state of Mankind. But why should we not assume, in accordance with the latest scientific view of Mankind in a state of anthropogenesis, that the parousiac spark can, of physical and organic necessity, only be kindled between Heaven and a mankind which has biologically reached a certain critical evolutionary point of collective maturity . . . For if truly, in order that the Kingdom of God may come . . . it is necessary, as an essential physical condition, that the human Earth should have already attained the natural completion of its evolutionary growth, then it must mean that the ultra-human perfection which neo-humanism envisages for Evolution will coincide in concrete terms with the crowning of the Incarnation awaited by all Christians.[131]

Here is a Christian gospel that would have a great attracting power to the neo-humanists of our day, and that would introduce a fruitful unity into the lives of contemporary Christians. If Teilhard presents the case in the above passage for Christian dedication to progress, the following statement from *The Divine Milieu* summarizes his argument for the importance of their efforts, also, to further human unity: "The only human embrace capable of worthily enfolding the divine is that of all men opening their arms to call down and welcome the fire." [132] The calling down of the fire is the most important requirement, for only an exceeding desire, enkindled in us by the Spirit at every Eucharistic celebration, can "merit" the final and totally gratuitous completion of our world at the Parousia. "The Lord Jesus will only come soon if we ardently expect Him. It is an accumulation of desires that should cause the Pleroma to burst upon us." [133]

The Pleroma will "burst upon us." Christ will not come from afar, from outside the space-time cone of cosmogenesis. If we picture mankind as having to leap a gap at the Parousia in order to reach Omega, it is only to signify the absolute gratuity of Christ's union with us at the Parousia. "For nothing can come to Christ unless he himself takes it and gathers it into himself." [134] But since Christ-Omega has immersed Himself in the cosmos and has so thoroughly and delicately penetrated it, suranimating cosmogenesis from within, the Parousia will mark that moment when He shall have so assimilated the universe into His Body that He can no longer restrain the full revelation of His glorious presence filling all things. It is literally Christ Himself who will "burst upon us," lifting us up forever with Him in the ecstatic Trinitarian Community and establishing us in the totally new and transcendent order of eternal glory. Teilhard describes this final moment very movingly in the following excerpt from an essay entitled "My Universe," which also provides a beautiful summary of his Christology.

And no doubt it is then, in a Creation brought to the paroxysm of its aptitude for union, that the Parousia will occur. The unique process

[132] *DM*, p. 124.
[133] *DM*, p. 134.
[134] "La Prêtre," *Ecrits*, pp. 285-302, (unpubl.), in *HU*, p. 152.

of assimilation and synthesis, pursued from the beginning of time, being at length revealed, the universal Christ will appear like a flash of lightning amid the storm clouds of a slowly consecrated World.

The trumpets of the angels are but a weak symbol. It is in the grip of the most powerful organic attraction conceivable (the force which held the Universe together!) that the monads will pour into that place whither they are irrevocably destined by the total maturing of all things and the implacable irreversibility of the whole history of the World—some of them spiritualized matter in the limitless fulfillment of an eternal communion, and others materialized spirit in the conscious agonies of an interminable decomposition.

At this moment, St. Paul tells us (I Cor. 15:23ff), when Christ shall have emptied of themselves all the powers created (rejecting that which is an element of dissociation and super-animating all that is the force of unity) He will consummate the universal unification by delivering Himself in His entire adult body, with a capacity for union that is at length perfected, to the embrace of the Deity.

Then the organic complex will have been constituted of God and the World, the Pleroma—the mysterious reality that we cannot do better than call simply God, since although God might dispense with the world we cannot regard it as being wholly an accessory without rendering Creation incomprehensible, the Passion of Christ meaningless, and our own struggle uninteresting.

Et tunc erit finis. [And then will be the end.]

Like a vast tide the Being will have dominated the trembling of all beings. The extraordinary venture of the World will have ended in the bosom of a tranquil ocean, of which, however, each drop will still be conscious of being itself. The dream of every mystic will have found its full and proper fulfillment. Erit in omnibus omnia Deus [God will be all in all].[135]

[135] *FM*, pp. 307-8.

CHAPTER THREE

The Sanctified Labor of Co-Creative Union

The Role of Human Labor in Christogenesis

In the first chapter we asked how and why human labor contributed to noogenesis. If we find ourselves somewhat overwhelmed by the importance which Teilhard's cosmogenesis gives to our human endeavor, how much more shall we wonder in amazement—and adoration—as we see the meaning and value of the same labor when it becomes the divinized instrument of Christogenesis.

It is through the collaboration which He stimulates in us that Christ, starting from *all* created things, is consummated and attains His plenitude. St. Paul himself tells us so. We may, perhaps, imagine that the creation was finished long ago. But that would be quite wrong. It continues still more magnificently, and at the highest levels of the world . . . And we serve to complete it, even by the humblest work of our hands. That is, ultimately, the meaning and value of our acts. Owing to the interrelation between matter, soul and Christ, we bring part of the being which He desires back to God *in whatever we do*. With each one of our *works*, we labour—in individual separation, but no less really—to build the Pleroma; that is to say, we bring to Christ a little fulfillment." [1]

We "bring to Christ a little fulfillment"; we "build the Pleroma." In some mysterious way, as we already noted, God needs the Pleroma; He "is completely self-sufficient, and yet the universe brings to Him something vitally necessary." [2] "Because of the

[1] *DM*, pp. 30-31.
[2] "Christianisme et évolution" (unpubl.), quoted in Mooney, p. 176.

Incarnation God can no longer do without the many among whom He has immersed Himself—at least from now on in the present order." [3] The very love which "compelled" Him to begin the creative act of Pleromization requires Him to fulfill it as "a mutual completion of [Himself] and the world"; [4] and for this completion He needs our collaboration.

Christ is not yet fully formed; he has not yet gathered about him the last folds of his robe of flesh and love which is made up of his faithful followers. The mystical Christ has not yet attained to his full growth; and therefore the same is true of the cosmic Christ. Both of these are simultaneously in the state of being and of becoming; and it is from the prolongation of this process of becoming *that all created activity ultimately springs.* Christ is the end point of evolution, even the *natural* evolution of all beings; and therefore evolution is holy." [5]

It is because evolution is holy, a Christogenesis, that Teilhard concludes "there is a hallowed *opus humanum*" [6] leading ultimately to the mystical effort presented in *The Divine Milieu*, which we might call a mysticism of co-creative union. God needs our cooperation to complete His Christ. Christ needs it to fulfill His Body through which He can totally express Himself in the created "other," and He needs our "help" simply because by the nature of the world He is creating, "He willed that He should have need of it." [7] "That the Kingdom of God arrive it is necessary that man conquer the earth," that it may "become the divinized cosmic Body of Christ." [8] In a sense, then, the Parousia of Christ will come as soon as we get the world ready for it, and it is the entire gamut of human labor Christified that is needed to prepare "the more or less proximate matter to be transformed into His Plenitude." [9] "Christ needs a summit of the world for His consummation just as He needed to find a woman for His

---

[3] "La Route de l'ouest" (unpubl.), p. 20, quoted in Mooney, p. 174.

[4] "Contingence de l'univers et gout humain de survivre" (unpubl.), pp. 3-4, quoted in Mooney, p. 174.

[5] "La Vie Cosmique," *Écrits*, pp. 5-61, in *HU*, p. 58. (Emphasis added.)

[6] Letter of July 26, 1917, in de Lubac, *The Religion . . .*, p. 248.

[7] *DM*, p. 39.

[8] "La Vie Cosmique," *Écrits*, p. 51.

[9] Letter of December 12, 1919, in *Archives de Philosophie* XXIV (1961), p. 140, quoted in Mooney, p. 151.

conception," [10] and it is *we*, empowered by His Spirit, who must bring the world to its summit of unity by immersing ourselves in and Christifying "the whole of the world's industrial, aesthetic, scientific and moral endeavour." [11] Such labors to bring to completion Christ's Body will revive, incarnate, and constantly intensify our expectation of the final appearance of the Lord. This expectancy, Teilhard says, "is perhaps the supreme Christian function and the most distinctive characteristic of our religion." [12] Our "Come, Lord Jesus!" must be expressed more and more in dedicated labor inspired by the conviction that "the greater man becomes, the more humanity becomes united, with consciousness of, and mastery of, its potentialities, the more beautiful creation will be, the more perfect adoration will become, and the more Christ will find, for mystical extensions, a body worthy of resurrection." [13] Then will Our Lord "change our lowly [yet cosmic-in-extent] body, to be like his glorious body, by the power which enables him to subject all things to himself." [14] In short, "to desire the Parousia [and so to hasten its coming], all we have to do is let the very heart of the earth, as we Christianize it, beat within us." [15] This is the truth we are to do in love until we attain to "the fullness of Christ." [16]

Precisely *how* is it that "the humblest work of our hands" serves to "build the Pleroma" and "bring to Christ a little fulfillment?" Again, we only need to transfuse with Christian revelation Teilhard's theory of noogenesis to see that the universe is drawn first into the faith-informed co-reflection of Christians, united in their communion of love, and is then assumed *in them*, into personal communion with Christ. It is only the personalized world that can be united in Christ. The universe will not become the total glorified Body of Christ until it has become the cosmic body of a totalized and unified mankind, and for this end the

10 "Comment je crois," (unpubl.), p. 23, n. 2, quoted in Mooney, pp. 61-62.
11 "A Note on Progress," *FM*, p. 23.
12 *DM*, pp. 134-135.
13 *DM*, p. 137.
14 Phil. 3:21 (RSV).
15 *DM*, p. 137.
16 Eph. 4: 15, 13 (RSV).

Christian must labor. In *The Divine Milieu,* Teilhard explains the process in a simple syllogism.[17] The major premise is an indisputable statement consistent both with traditional theology and with Teilhard's cosmogenesis: "At the heart of our universe each soul exists for God in Our Lord." The universe culminates in persons called into existence for personal union with their Creator who knew them each by name before they were conceived from the very beginning of cosmogenesis. Each one's essential meaning lies in a unique relationship with Christ-Omega towards whom their personal evolution has been directed, and in whom they are to become centered and totalized. The end of the world, Teilhard explains, will be attained by "the realization of an organic unity—into which, of course, will be drawn the whole marvelous essence of the inter-personal relationships that characterize the Universe, starting with Man." [18] Without losing their own personalities and sustained in a complex network of perfected interpersonal relationships, each is to become so completely identified with Christ that all together they manifest and express fully the personality of Christ the Word. St. Paul's "I live now not I . . ." will be the unanimous experience of the parousiac community, and it is this cry of union in vision that will be the final and everlasting "hymn of the universe."

Teilhard's minor premise is that "all reality, even material reality around each of us, exists for our souls." For "we live at the center of a network of cosmic influences" and our roots "plunge back and down into the unfathomable past." Our souls are "besieged and penetrated by a flow of cosmic influences which have to be ordered and assimilated" as they "pass through our consciousness" and "merge into the most intimate life of our soul," serving there as the force by which we shape our own unique personality with its "characteristic power of understanding and loving." Thus each one of us sums up in himself, and so spiritualizes and personalizes, in his own unique and incommunicable way, the whole world. When Christ incorporates us into Himself, He assumes "our" world, also, and when all men have be-

[17] *DM*, pp. 25-31.
[18] Letter of April 29, 1934, quoted in de Lubac, *T. de C. the Man . . . ,* p. 154.

come one in the unanimous synthesis and personalization of the universe which will mark the final maturation of mankind, Christ will unite to Himself the whole material universe assimilated to the optimum into the souls of men. It is a union of persons whom Christ draws into Himself first and foremost, and then the material world which has helped to shape the persons as they personalized it and made it their own collective and cosmic body.[19] Or, to put it more simply, it is the world of multiplicity united in mankind, in the Christian communion, that finally is assumed into the perfect oneness of divine union and constitutes the Pleroma. "This," Teilhard summarizes, "is *the general 'drift'* of matter towards spirit. This movement must have its term: one day the whole divinizable substance of matter will have passed into the souls of men; all the chosen dynamism will have been recuperated and then our world will be ready for the Parousia." [20]

That part of the material universe that has been or can be assimilated into man, into his understanding or into that web of interpersonal relationships that make up his unity, is what Teilhard calls the *chosen* or divinizable part, and it is this, the Body of Christ in its state of becoming, that constitutes *the world that he loves.* This is the key to understanding Teilhard's religious, even mystical, drive "to extract from this world all it can hold of truth and energy" and also his theory of the spiritual power of matter.[21] Explaining his joint "passion for the world and passion for God," Teilhard writes to his cousin Marguerite to whom he revealed most intimately his own interior life:

What I appreciate in the earth is obviously not its lower part, now outstripped and decrepit . . . For me the real earth is that chosen part of the universe, still almost universally dispersed and in course of gradual segregation, but which is, little by little, taking on body and form in Christ.[22]

True human progress, a "supernatural" extension of noogenesis, consists, therefore, in subjecting to mankind that *chosen* part of matter which "because it has been assimilated into the Body of

19 *DM*, pp. 27-30.
20 *DM*, p. 86.
21 Letter of August 4, 1916, *MM*, p. 116.
22 Letter of January 19, 1917, *MM*, p. 165.

Christ . . . is destined to pass into the foundations and walls of the heavenly Jerusalem." [23] Thus it is that "through an effort (even a purely natural effort) to learn the truth, to live the good, to create the beautiful; through cutting away all inferior and evil energies; through practicing that charity towards all men which alone can gather up the multitude into a single soul," in order "*to promote*, in however small a degree, the *awakening of spirit in the world*," the Christian laborer offers to the Incarnate Word some part of the whole world in his soul.[24]

The conclusion of Teilhard's syllogism is obvious, and it brings us back to the point with which we opened this examination of Teilhard's spirituality: "All sensible reality, around each one of us, exists through our souls, for God in Our Lord." Thus,

Little by little, stage by stage, everything is finally linked to the supreme Center *in quo omnia constant*. The emanations coming from this Center operate not only within the higher zones of the world, where human activities take place in a distinctively super-natural and meritorious form. In order to save and constitute these sublime energies, the power of the Incarnate Word penetrates matter itself; it descends into the deepest depths of the inferior forces. And the Incarnation will be complete only when the part of chosen substance contained in every object—spiritualized first of all in our souls and a second time with our souls in Jesus—has rejoined the final Center of its completion. *Quid est quod ascendit, nisi quod prius descendit, ut repleret omnia* [He who descended is also he who ascended, that he might fill all things].

It is through the collaboration which He stimulates in us that Christ, starting from *all* created things, is consummated and attains His plenitude.[25]

The Spirituality and Mysticism of Co-Creative Union

The heart of Teilhard's spirituality flows directly from his theory of creative-union. It is no more nor less than the intimate union with Christ which is the essence of Gospel and Pauline

[23] "La Vie Cosmique," *Ecrits*, pp. 53-4, quoted in Mooney, p. 149.
[24] "Le Prêtre," *Ecrits*, pp. 285-302, *HU*, p. 60.
[25] *DM*, pp. 30-31. [Eng. trans. from *RSV*, Eph. 4:10.]

spirituality, conceived of as a union of co-creation or co-redemption (the two dimensions, ultimately, of one unitive operation). Union with the Father and the Son—who are working "even until now"—can only be a *co*-creative union activated by the power of the Spirit working in us. The more we are drawn into Christ and the more all our powers are focused on Him in love, the more we are compelled by this very love to labor for the building up of His Body. The charity of Christ urges us on, Paul tells us, for only when all Christians, the *chosen*, have filled up in themselves what is yet lacking in the creative and redemptive work of the Cross, will Christ "burst forth upon us." Conversely, the more I labor faithfully, disinterestedly, even passionately, to conquer "my world" for Christ, the more deeply His Presence will penetrate into me (and "my world"). In a passage that seems to flow joyously from deep prayer, Teilhard writes:

In action I cleave to the creative power of God; I coincide with it; I become not only its instrument but its living prolongation. And since there is nothing more personal in a being than its will, I merge myself, in a sense, through my heart, with the very heart of God. This contact is continuous because I am always acting; and at the same time, since I can never find a limit to the perfection of my fidelity or the fervour of my intention, it enables me to assimilate myself still more narrowly, and indefinitely, to God.[26]

Thus *every* work, "even in the realms inaccurately called profane," must, in the Christian life, assume the role of a holy and unifying operation. "It is the collaboration, trembling with love, which we give to the hands of God," as He prepares us and the world for final union.[27] Co-laboring consciously with God to build the Pleroma is a new and unifying way of adoration which involves and centers on God the whole of our lives. It is an adoration which "means the giving of our body and soul to creative activity, joining that activity to Him to bring the world to fulfillment by effort and research."[28] Once our "eyes are opened" to the divine milieu and we realize that God unites with us in our labors, not because we are doing blindly some "busy-

[26] *DM*, pp. 31-32.
[27] *DM*, p. 71.
[28] "Christologie et évolution" (unpubl.). p. 12.

work" to please Him, but because He and we are collaborating to achieve an end which we see and desire together, then we cannot fail to be overwhelmed not only by "the boundless joy of creation" [29] but by the immeasurably greater joy of mystical co-creation.

Our union with God in our action does not in the least lessen any of the human aspect of our action: "The tremendous power of the divine attraction is focused on our frail desires and the microscopic intents without breaking their points. It suranimates; hence it neither disturbs nor stifles anything." [30] "No, God does not deflect our gaze prematurely from the work He Himself has given us, since He presents Himself to us as attainable through that very work." [31] It is only by pursuing our works with the utmost of human perfection demanded by them that we shall discover God "waiting for us at every moment in our action . . . at the tip of my pen, my spade, my brush, my needle—of my heart and of my thought." [32] Even our loving awareness of His presence cannot excuse us from the greatest human exactitude in the task at hand for "Christian faith destroys neither man's rational mode of conquering the world nor his confidence in himself." Rather, "it brings to human effort, which it takes great care to preserve as a foundation, an unexpected completion; it directs it, organizes it and finally transforms it." [33] "Hence whatever our role as men may be, whether we are artists, workingmen or scholars," [34] we must ever be going *"with haste into the hill country,"* even though we are going *with Him.*

The soul does not pause to enjoy this communion, nor does it lose sight of the material end of its action; it is wedded to a *creative* effort. The will to succeed, a certain passionate delight in the work to be done, form an integral part of our creaturely fidelity. It follows that the very sincerity with which we desire and pursue success for God reveals itself as a new factor—also without limits—in our more perfect conjunction with the All-powerful who animates us. Originally

[29] Letter of April 8, 1930, *LT,* p. 164.
[30] *DM,* p. 34.
[31] *DM,* p. 33.
[32] *DM,* p. 33.
[33] "La foi qui opère," *Ecrits,* p. 235, quoted in Mooney, p. 208.
[34] *DM,* p. 32.

associated with God in the simple common exercise of wills, we now unite ourselves to Him in a common love of the end for which we are working; and the crowning marvel is that, with the possession of this end, we have the utter joy of discovering His presence once again.[35]

Our experience of co-creative union, however, will develop in us an exquisite delicacy of conscience, a complete dependence on God, and an earnest fidelity to the human demands of each moment.

Anyone who has this insight [of God's creative power acting on us and through us], and who loves, will feel within himself a fever of active dependence and/or arduous purity seizing upon him and driving him on to an absolute integrity and the complete utilization of all his powers.

In order to become perfectly resonant to the pulsations of the basic rhythm of reality the mystic makes himself docile to the least hint of human obligation, the most unobtrusive demands of grace.[36]

It is in the human task confronting us at this moment, that Christ offers Himself to us, and we can unite with Him only by co-laboring with Him in that work, offering Him the sacrifice of our innate tendencies to a comfortable and selfish inertia in order to bring to Him in this small effort "a little fulfillment." Without this fidelity to our fundamental vocation, our professed love of God will be a "clanging cymbal." The only genuine response of love we can give to the indwelling Father, Son, and Spirit is to unite with them in ardently pursuing the final unification which they are pursuing with divine passion, for love of us. "Not everyone who says to me, 'Lord, Lord' . . . but he who does the will of my Father . . ."[37] and what is the Father's will but that we co-labor with the Spirit to complete the cosmic Body of His Son. Fidelity is the incarnation of our love and the only worthy "return to the Lord" for the Incarnation of His love for which we are called into being.

Through fidelity we situate ourselves and maintain ourselves in the hands of God so exactly as to become one with them in their action.

[35] *DM*, p. 32.

[36] "La Lutte contre la Multitude," *Ecrits*, pp. 113-32, in *HU*, p. 118.

[37] Matt. 7, 21. Cf. "Constitution on Church in Modern World," art. 93, Abbott, p. 307.

Through fidelity we open ourselves so intimately and continually to the wishes and good pleasure of God, that His life penetrates and assimilates ours like a fortifying bread . . . Through fidelity and fidelity alone can we return to God the kiss He is for ever offering us across the world.[38]

Even as our collaboration with God will prompt us to perform our work with increasing human perfection, it will at the same time urge us to an ever more complete dependence on Him. Teilhard advises his cousin Marguerite:

I think that the time has come for you resolutely to set the activity of our Lord at the center of your influence,—to count for the full success of your work primarily on your own degree of union with the presence and will of the master.

When you suffer and toil, what you are doing is simply to attach your own small effort to him who is the soul of all creation, [for] he alone can give *real existence* to what our actions produce.[39]

It is our growing union with Christ in our work that will deepen our realization that together we are co-laboring in a work that only He can achieve. Whether it is a matter of our individual accomplishment of some small task confronting us here and now, or the completion of the whole collective task of mankind, "the triumph of progress will come from God, under the form of His providence, at His own appointed time, and in excess of our own expectations. The worker who puts his confidence in God knows that neither endeavor nor aspiration is lost if it is done in grace; they reach their goal because they pass through the living Center of every useful activity." [40]

The Renunciation
Inherent in Fidelity to Co-Creative Union

It should be apparent that in Teilhard's spirituality of co-creative union "a true and deep renunciation lies concealed." [41] Teilhard's love of the world and dedication to human progress is,

[38] *DM*, pp. 118-19.
[39] *MM*, pp. 62, 86, 210.
[40] "La Maîtrise du monde et le Règne de Dieu," *Ecrits*, pp. 82-3, quoted in Mooney, p. 11.
[41] *DM*, p. 40.

in fact, the most authentic and exacting form of Christian detachment. The man who appears to be attached to his work is, by his very attachment, almost forced along the way of greater detachment.

In the first place it [work] implies effort and a victory over inertia. And then, however interesting and intellectual it may be (and the more intellectual it is, the truer this becomes) work is always accompanied by the painful pangs of birth . . . To create, or organize material energy, or truth, or beauty, brings with it an inner torment which prevents those who face its hazards from sinking into the quiet and closed-in life wherein grows the vice of egoism and attachment. An honest workman not only surrenders his tranquility and peace once and for all, but must learn to abandon over and over again the form which his labour or art or thought first took, and go in search of new forms. To pause, so as to enjoy or possess results, would be a betrayal of action. Over and over again he must transcend himself, tear himself away from himself, leaving behind him his most cherished beginnings.[42]

The cross that Christ requires His followers to carry after Him every day is first of all the inescapable depth-dimension of our fidelity to the human and Christian task of building the Earth, the Body of Christ. Thus, "the formula for renunciation," Teilhard explains, to his friend Father Auguste Valensin, "if it is to be total, must satisfy two conditions:

1. It must enable us to go beyond everything there is in the world.
2. And yet at the same time compel us to press forward (with conviction and passion—because it is a question of life or death) to the development of this same world." [43]

He immediately points out the basic premise, which we have examined in chapter two, on which he bases his understanding of renunciation:

I think that detachment and attachment, these two properties which are contradiciory in appearance and which make up the complete Christian attitude, harmonize quite easily, provided one agrees that the supernatural Pleroma grows out of the natural universe according to a law of transformation, not one of rupture.—Transformation, in

[42] *DM*, p. 41.
[43] *Correspondence*, p. 33.

that the supernatural actually rearranges the elements of this world, to the point of making them truly *more* and *other than they were*— but also transformation in the sense that the natural elements are absolutely necessary to this work of salvation, providing it with its fuel and with a suitable material. The supernatural fullness of Christ depends upon the natural fullness of the world.[44]

Regarding the relative value of growth or diminishment, possession or renunciation, Teilhard answers:

Why separate and contrast the two natural phases of a single effort? Your essential duty and desire is to be united with God. But in order to be united, you must first of all *be*—be yourself as completely as possible. And so you must develop yourself and take possession of the world *in order to be*. Once this has been accomplished, then is the time to think about renunciation; then is the time to accept diminishment for the sake of *being in another*.[45]

Accordingly, in reply to Marguerite's worry about how to practice "renunciation in the midst of activity," Teilhard writes:

But you answer this for yourself: by action! The greatest sacrifice we can make, the greatest victory we can win over ourselves, is to surmount inertia, the tendency to follow the line of least resistance. Christian action, by its very nature, both detaches one and unites one to our Lord. Without bothering yourself about theoretical renunciations, begin by devoting yourself to the task, often thankless, assigned to you BY GOD.[46]

We must remember that the world that Teilhard loves is the "chosen part," as he indicates in the remark to Marguerite: "I always think that there's a way of being detached by so attaching oneself to that element in the world that breaks away and becomes divinized." [47] This divinizable substance we can extract from the material world only by progressing along a way that leads ever upwards toward "the highest possible spiritualization by means of the greatest possible effort," [48] which is, in fact, as we have seen, the way of the Cross. Teilhard explains:

[44] *Ibid.*
[45] *DM*, p. 70.
[46] Letter of July 4, 1915, *MM*, p. 58.
[47] Letter of January 18, 1917, *MM*, p. 172.
[48] *DM*, p. 77.

Anyone whose aim, in conquering the earth, has really been to subject a little more matter to spirit, has, surely, begun to take leave of himself at the same time as taking possession of himself. This is also true of the man who rejects mere enjoyment, the line of least resistance, the easy possession of things and ideas, and sets out courageously on the path of work, inward renewal and the ceaseless broadening and purification of his ideal.[49]

"To rise above the world, therefore, does not mean to despise or reject it, but to pass through it and sublime [sic] it." [50] True Christian detachment is not so much a going against as a going beyond. It demands, however, an absolute renunciation of oneself, one's "personal success or personal satisfaction," a renunciation which Teilhard sees as a threshold (a conversion), that must be crossed before we can experience the joyous "freedom to work and to love" with and for God alone.[51] To acquire this "freedom of the children of God" means that "in the present struggle each of us must forget what he might acquire of selfish personal improvement to become just part of the single effort devoted to the common task." [52] The balance between detachment and attachment, self-development and self-renunciation which should characterize the Christian life is only authentic if the attachment and self-development are always pursued "with a view to transcending," of climbing ever higher, and therefore are in themselves, "something penetrated and dominated by detachment." [53] Some of the time-tested practices of Christian penance or self-denial may be useful "to organize the hierarchy of, and liberate the lower forces" within us, and even purify of self-seeking our positive efforts, though in the latter case, the only really effective antidote is the contemplation of *"the Greater than All."* [54] Teilhard realized the importance of getting beneath the surface in our renunciation and proposes that exercises in detachment should be designed so as "to shatter the narrowness

49 *DM*, p. 72.
50 "Some Reflections on Progress," *FM*, p. 79.
51 Letter of October 30, 1929, *LT*, p. 160.
52 Letter of July 27, 1915, *MM*, p. 61.
53 *DM*, p. 70.
54 *DM*, pp. 73, 72.

of one's views, one's desires, one's egoism." [55] The accelerating
rate of progress that characterizes our transitional era with its
demands for a constant openness to new ideas and conflicting
views, would seem to provide us with abundant exercises in that
sort of detachment. Whatever other exercises in renunciation we
perform, they are *for the sake of* forming in us a general habit of
disinterested and exacting fidelity to our great Christian task of
co-creation, which constitutes in itself the higher and more genuine detachment of Christian action.

The Necessity for Faith: Devotion to Prayer and the Eucharist

Our constant efforts to become ever more detached from
selfish interest and laziness in our work prepare us for an ever
more intense and refined faith and purity, which are two essential
qualities of the God-centered intention which alone can transform our human works into direct instruments of Pleromization.
The progress of noogenesis, we have seen, is absolutely contin-
gent on man's growth in consciousness; it is by his increasing co-
reflective synthesis that he assimilates the universe into his collective cosmic vision as he becomes more and more consciously
centered on Omega and simultaneously unified within himself.
Having been transformed by the Incarnation into Christogenesis,
man's progress depends, ultimately, on his synthesizing the
world in his faith-informed vision of the Cosmic Christ. Spirit-
empowered faith opens the Christian and "his world" to the
pleromizing Spirit that radiates from Christ-Omega, the divine
Center, permeating and transforming the universe even as the sun
pervades the solar system with its life-giving rays; and purity
makes him a transparent medium of the transforming grace of
Christ. Faith opens our eyes to the full Christic dimension of
cosmogenesis; it enables us to see Christ, who is Himself the
divine milieu in which creative union is accomplished: Christ-
Omega, lifted up by His Resurrection and drawing all things to

[55] Quoted in de Lubac, *T. de C., the Man* . . . , p. 119.

Himself through His Eucharistic action. Supernatural faith also "sensitizes" the Christian to the operative power of the divine milieu, or in other words, activates him with the power of Christ's creative Spirit. Without a faith-informed intention, our works can at best only indirectly serve to achieve the unity in Christ which is the totally gratuitous end of the redeemed world. Even agnostics and the irreligious, however unconsciously and involuntarily, "collaborate in the Kingdom of God and in the fulfillment of the elect"; for, "their efforts transcending or correcting their incomplete or bad intentions, are gathered in by Him 'whose energy subjects all things to itself.' But that is no more than second best . . . Right from the hands that knead the dough, to those that consecrate it," Teilhard writes poetically, "the great and universal Host should be prepared and handled in a spirit of adoration." [56] The more intense the faith and purity of our intention, the more "our action is animated by grace," and therefore the more "it builds up to a true Body, that of Christ, who wished to be completed through each one of us." [57] Thus, our intention transforms our work into the "redemptive incarnation" of our love of Christ who "is and who is to come." [58]

Our good intention is, in fact, the "necessary start and foundation of all else . . . it is the golden key which unlocks our personal world to God's presence. It is true that "the divinization of our endeavor by the value of the intention put into it, pours a priceless *soul* into all our actions," [59] even though it is not the intention itself that confers the "hope of resurrection on their bodies," but rather the reality on which the intention is founded, that is, that the products of our labors themselves are destined to become incorporated into the glorified Body of Christ. Teilhard summarizes very succinctly the role of intention in transforming both the product and the process of our labor, in the two following statements: "Our total human effort, the more it is done with a good intention, collaborates toward the fullness of the Incarna-

[56] *DM*, p. 36.
[57] "La Vie Cosmique," *Ecrits*, p. 41, quoted in Mooney, p. 149.
[58] Apoc. 1, 8.
[59] *DM*, p. 23.

tion." [60] "And the combined power of faith and intention . . .
reveals to the Christian a zone at the heart of the universe in
which *quidquid patimur, Christus patitur; quidquid agimus,
Christus agitur*." [Whatever we suffer, Christ suffers; whatever
we do, Christ does.] [61]

We must examine more closely the faith and purity which
characterize this intention that opens to us the divine milieu, and
which form, together with fidelity, the three "operatives" by
which the power of the divine milieu invades our lives.[62] As one
of these "operatives," faith both compels and enables us to join in
the continuous act by which Christ, "through the magnetism of
His love and the effective power of His Eucharist, gradually
gathers into Himself all the unitive energy scattered throughout
His creation." [63] For, enlightened by faith, we are drawn into co-
creative union first in the intense moment of Eucharistic contact
with Christ-Omega, and then in our every human act suranimated by His Spirit and empowered to transmit His unitive grace
to all that we touch.

In our hands, in the hands of all of us, the world and life (*our world,
our life*) are placed like a Host, ready to be charged with the divine
influence, that is to say with a real Presence of the Incarnate Word.
The mystery will be accomplished. But on one condition: which is
that *we shall believe* that *this* has the will and the power to become
for us the action—that is to say the prolongation of the Body of
Christ.[64]

Thus, "if we have faith, the irresistible forces of life and matter
really become for us the organizing action of Christ assimilating
us to Himself." [65]

The faith which alone can open to us the divine milieu, and
reveal to us the world "charged with Jesus," [66] leads us necessar-

[60] "L'Element Universel," *Ecrits*, p. 411, quoted in Mooney, p. 150.
[61] "Forma Christi," *Ecrits*, p. 344, quoted in Mooney, p. 150.
[62] *DM*, p. 112.
[63] "La Lutte contre la Multitude," *Ecrits*, pp. 113-32, in *HU*, p. 119.
[64] *DM*, pp. 116-117.
[65] "L'Element Universel," *Ecrits*, p. 411, quoted in Mooney, p. 150.
[66] de Lubac, p. 158.

ily to that activity through which faith is received and intensified, to the highest activity, therefore, possible to man, to prayer.

The perception of the divine omnipresence is essentially a seeing, a taste, that is to say a sort of intuition bearing upon certain superior qualities in things. It cannot therefore, be attained directly by any artifice. It is a gift, like life itself, of which it is undoubtedly the supreme experimental perfection . . . God tends, by the logic of His creative effort, to make Himself sought and perceived by us: *Posuit homines . . . si forte attrectent eum* [He made men . . . that they might reach out to him]. His prevenient grace is therefore always on the alert to excite our first look and our first prayer. But in the end the initiative, the awakening, always come from Him, and whatever the further developments of our mystical faculties, no progress is achieved in this domain except as the new response to a new gift. *Nemo venit ad me, nisi Pater traxerit eum* [No one comes to me, unless the Father draws him].

We are thus led to posit intense and continual prayer at the origin of our invasion by the divine milieu, the prayer which begs for the fundamental gift: *Domine, fac ut videam* [Lord, that I may see]. Lord, we know and feel that You are everywhere around us; but it seems that there is a veil before our eyes. *Illumina vultum tuum super nos* [Shine your countenance upon us]—let the light of Your countenance shine upon us in its universality. *Sit splendor Domini nostri super nos* [Let the splendor of our Lord be upon us]—may Your deep brilliance light up the innermost parts of the massive obscurities in which we move. And, to that end, send us Your spirit, *Spiritus principalis*, whose flaming action alone can operate the birth and achievement of the great metamorphosis which sums up all inward perfection and towards which Your creation yearns: *Emitte Spiritum tuum, et creabuntur, et RENOVABIS FACIEM TERRAE* [Send forth your Spirit, and they shall be created, and you shall renew the face of the earth].[67]

There is no possibility, therefore, of imputing to Teilhard a false activism, nor of using his ideas as an excuse for activism. He insists that:

There are, of course, certain noble and cherished moments of the day—those when we pray or receive the sacraments. But for these moments of more efficient or more explicit contact, the tide of the

[67] *DM*, pp. 111-112.

divine omnipresence, and our perception of it, would weaken until all that was best in our human endeavour, without being entirely lost to the world, would be for us emptied of God. But once we have jealously safeguarded our relation to God encountered, if I may dare use the expression, 'in a pure state' (that is to say in a state of Being distinct from all the elements of this world), there is no need to fear that the most banal, absorbing or attractive of occupations should force us to depart from Him. To repeat: by virtue of the Creation and, still more, of the Incarnation, *nothing* here below *is profane* for those who know how to see.[68]

Teilhard's letters to Marguerite whom he calls the companion of his search [69] and to whom he reveals his own spiritual life most intimately are filled with this repeated insistence on the value and necessity of prayer.

You could hardly believe how vividly when I have a chance to collect myself a little and think and pray . . . I become aware of the growing light of this truth, so simple and yet so infinitely rich and fruitful, that God is all.[70]

We must pray for one another, then, that our Lord may keep us both humble and fearless, supremely united above all to his divinity, the source of every fruitful activity.[71]

Interior recollection, a certain ascesis, are matchless forces, even for natural human development.[72]

After an exhausting battle at Verdum he writes:

Between now and Friday I'm going to try to bring myself as close as possible . . . to the heart of our Lord. My need is great to steep my soul in him again, so that I may have more faith, more devotion, more kindness.[73]

We glimpse the manner in which Teilhard "steeped" his soul in Christ from the following reflection in a letter written on the Feast of the Presentation:

[68] *DM*, p. 35.
[69] Letter of January 9, 1917, *MM*, p. 166.
[70] Letter of December 24, 1915, *MM*, p. 84.
[71] Letter of September 18, 1916, *MM*, p. 128.
[72] Letter of January 14, 1919, *MM*, p. 278.
[73] Letter of June 25, 1916, *MM*, p. 105.

We often say to God, 'I give myself to you, I wish to unite myself to you.' We say this sincerely, but do we not forget that it is he alone who can give himself and raise a being to some small degree of union with himself? The attitude that incorporates us fully with the truth is indeed that of the Presentation, in which we humbly expose ourselves to the radiation of the infinite Being, ardently longing that he may penetrate us and transform us into himself.[74]

It was from such prayer that Teilhard learned both his humble dependence on Christ that was the heart of his "detachment in action" and his "impassioned desire to help forward the synthesis of Christ and the universe." [75] Recalling St. Margaret Mary's experience of being unable to unite with Christ until He drew her into Himself, Teilhard tells Marguerite:

In this account I recognize the two elements which sum up life for me: *absolute dependence* on the creative and sanctifying energy of God, which alone can maintain rooted in us the passion for life, the passion for God;—and then, once this deep-seated attraction has been implanted in us, *an invasion by the divinity* of our whole environment, of all that we do, so that for us everything becomes self-giving, transforming God.[76]

Teilhard's prayer and his whole life was as Christo-centric as his theological synthesis. His love for the person of Christ as the Sacred Heart and as the Cosmic Christ complemented and completed each other and found their highest expression in His love of the Eucharist.[77] For him the Sacred Heart was "the master above all of the interior life." [78] He asks Marguerite: "While you are so close to our Lord, so responsive to the influence of His heart, you must ask him to give both of us a great love of his person, so that it may become the strength and joy of our life. Our Lord's heart is indeed ineffably beautiful and satisfying: it exhausts all reality." [79] A favorite prayer which he shares with Marguerite reveals the warmth and intimacy of his relationship with Christ:

[74] Letter of February 2, 1916, *MM*, p. 93.
[75] "Notes de Retraites" (unpubl.), quoted in *HU*, p. 100.
[76] Letter of March 13, 1917, *MM*, p. 192.
[77] Cf. de Lubac, *T. de C., the Man . . .*, pp. 43-77, 56ff.
[78] Letter of June 29, 1916, *MM*, p. 107.
[79] Letter of March 31, 1917, *MM*, p. 192.

And then, my Lord, enfold me in the depths of thy Heart.
And there keep me, refine, purge, kindle, set on fire, raise aloft,
according to the most pure desire of thy Heart,
and for my cleansing extinction.[80]

In the Heart of Jesus Teilhard discovers "all the length and
breadth and height and depth" of the Risen Lord of the Cosmos
to whom he can abandon himself in adoration. It is his vision of
the cosmic Christ that gives infinite breadth to his devotion to the
Sacred Heart, while the latter keeps his love of the great God of
the Universe very personal and intimate, as the following extracts
from one of his prayers so movingly illustrate:

Jesus . . . the humanity You put on in Palestine has gradually spread
to all parts, like a halo of countless colours, in which Your Presence
penetrated every other presence around me, super-animating it, never
destroying . . .

Lord of my childhood and of my end—*God, fulfilled for himself, and
yet for us, God whose birth has no end*—God who, since You offer
Yourself for our adoration as "evolver and evolutive," are now the
only God who can bring us satisfaction—tear away at last all the
clouds that still veil You.

And grant that, in diaphany and in flame, Your universal presence
may spring forth.[81]

This magnificent prayer from Teilhard's last years echoes a beautiful aspiration found in *The Divine Milieu:* "Greater still, Lord,
let Your universe be greater still, so that I may hold You and be
held by You by a ceaselessly widened and intensified contact!" [82]
In this age when much speculation on the meaning of the Eucharistic action and the universal Presence of Christ has led in
some circles to a lessening of devotion to the Eucharist, it is
particularly significant to note that Teilhard's mystical experience of Christ *everywhere* and especially in the human task of
each moment, as well as his entire synthesis of Christogenesis, led

[80] Letter of September 23, 1917, *MM*, p. 203; tr. in *HU*, p. 33 n.i.
[81] "Le Coeur de la Matière," (unpubl.), quoted in de Lubac, *T. de C. the
Man . . .*, pp. 44-45.
[82] *DM*, p. 15.

him not to diminish but to exalt to its rightful preeminence the Eucharistic Presence of Christ. The Eucharist in his thought is the most intense and dynamic point of contact with Christ-Omega, as we have already noted, and every other presence of Christ is but an extension of this Eucharistic presence. From the front he confides to Marguerite:

I carry the consecrated host on me, for the benefit of some of the Zouaves. And so I spend my day literally heart to heart with our Lord . . . May our Lord grant that this prolonged presence of his may enlighten our eyes and heart a little, as you too wish, so that we may see him in all things, more completely and really.[83]

In the Eucharistic action he sees summed up and mutually intensified the whole interrelated mystery of Christ's universal work of creative union and his own life of co-creative union in Him. Perhaps the clearest expression of this is his beautiful Eucharistic prayer in *The Divine Milieu* from which the following key lines have been taken:

Grant, O God, that when I draw near to the altar to communicate, I may henceforth discern the infinite perspectives hidden beneath the smallness and the nearness of the Host in which You are concealed . . .

I am beginning to understand: under the sacramental Species it is primarily through the 'accidents' of matter that You touch me, but, as a consequence, it is also through the whole universe in proportion as this ebbs and flows over me under Your primary influence. In a true sense the arms and the heart which You open to me are nothing less than all the united powers of the world which, penetrated and permeated to their depths by Your will, Your tastes and Your temperament, converge upon my being to form it, nourish it and bear it along towards the center of Your fire. In the host it is *my life* that You are offering me, O Jesus.

What can I do to gather up and answer that universal and enveloping embrace? . . . To the total offer that is made me, I can only answer by a total acceptance. I shall therefore *react* to the eucharistic contact with *the entire effort of my life*—of my life of today and of my life of tomorrow, of my personal life and of my life as linked to all other lives. Periodically, the sacred Species may perhaps fade away in me.

[83] Letter of March 27, 1916, *MM*, p. 96.

But each time they will leave me a little more deeply engulfed in the layers of Your omnipresence: living and dying. I shall never at any moment cease to move forward in You.[84]

Purity and Dependence: Devotion to Mary

It is the Eucharist invading his life that drives the Christian to serve Christ in his work and to expand his love of others with the greatest possible purity of heart. Purity "is the rectitude and impulse introduced into our lives by the love of God sought in and above everything." [85] In our work it shows itself in a pure intention to work solely for the love of Christ and His Body, linked with a confident dependence on His power operating through us to achieve this end which we seek *for Him*. This purity is essentially bound up with humble trust that God who has graciously made us His co-laborers will bring to a fulfillment "that eye has not seen" the small works of our hands. Basic to this trust is the conviction that the divinizing "flame can come only from above and that we'll be able to keep it burning only through purity and humility." [86] The need of purity for the unification of the world and the world's apparent lack of it becomes so clear to Teilhard that he tells Marguerite: "I pray to God with all my strength that He may make of you a most pure and docile instrument for His action. When once one has begun to see people and events in this particular light,—one can only be terrified at the crying need for purity that the universe suffers from, and almost beside oneself with longing to do something to supply it." [87] In another letter Teilhard describes this purity and indicates why it is so essential to the growth of the Pleroma:

He is spiritually impure who, lingering in pleasure or shut up in selfishness, introduces, within himself and around himself, a principle of slowing-down and division in the unification of the universe in God.

[84] *DM*, pp. 104-106.
[85] *DM*, p. 112.
[86] Letter of September 17, 1919, *MM*, p. 307.
[87] Letter of November 13, 1918, *MM*, p. 251.

He is pure, on the other hand, who, in accord with his place in the world, seeks to give Christ's desire to consummate all things precedence over his own immediate and momentary advantage.

Still purer and more pure is he who, attracted by God, succeeds in giving that movement and impulse of Christ's an even greater continuity, intensity and reality.[88]

Therefore, that the creative power of Christ's Spirit may operate more intensively through his activity, the Christian "labours unceasingly to purify his affections and to remove even the very faintest opacities which might cloud or impede the light." [89] For "if we want the divine milieu to grow all around us, then we must jealously guard and nourish all the forces of union, of desire, and of prayer that grace offers us. By the mere fact that our transparency will increase, the divine light, that never ceases to press in upon us, will erupt the more powerfully." [90] Purity assimilates all the human powers and passions into a single totalizing act, the love of Jesus, who is "at once God and everything"; and so its specific effect is "to unite the inner powers of the soul in an act of unique passion, rich and intense beyond words"—a passion for God.[91] Thus it is purity made fruitful by faith which unifies and hence spiritualizes the individual and prepares him for the divine embrace at death, just as charity will unite and lift up the whole of redeemed mankind to the total divine embrace at the Parousia.[92] And it is faith-inspired purity by which we open ourselves to God's penetrating and consuming glance, that allows Him to "concentrate Himself" within us "to the point of appearing" in our humanity as though by another epiphany.[93] Through the man who knows Him with a pure heart, Christ can partially but really express and manifest himself in a way that begins already to foreshadow his final and total manifestation in the Spirit-united community of the Parousia. Putting this in practical terms,

[88] DM, p. 113. (Emphasis added.)
[89] "Le Milieu mystique," Ecrits, pp. 137-167, quoted in HU, p. 118.
[90] DM, p. 114.
[91] "La Lutte contre la Multitude," Ecrits, pp. 113-32, quoted in de Lubac, T. de C., the Man . . ., p. 66.
[92] DM, pp. 114, 126.
[93] MM, pp. 149, 274.

Teilhard confides to Marguerite: "May our Lord unite us so thoroughly with himself that he may be seen in all that we do, above all through his kindness and his great love; this is what I ask for you, and for myself, and for all I love." [94]

The one from whom Teilhard asked for this grace of purity and in whom he found its perfect exemplar was Mary, the Mother of Christ. The Immaculate Conception Teilhard sees as "the feast of 'passive action,' the action that functions simply by the transmission through us of the divine." [95] God so penetrated our Lady's whole being from the moment of her conception that her personal life from its very beginning was characterized by the unity and simplicity of the God who would assume His humanity within her.

When the time had come when God resolved to realise His Incarnation before our eyes, He had first of all to raise up in the world a virtue capable of drawing Him as far as ourselves. He needed a mother who would engender Him in the human sphere. What did He do? He created the Virgin Mary, that is to say He called forth on earth a purity so great that, within this transparency, He would concentrate Himself to the point of appearing as a child.[96]

Teilhard adds: "May our Lord give you and me, too, a little of her translucence, which is so favorable to God's action." [97] Again, he prays "that God through our Lady may grant us to share in her purity and to have so ardent a passion for her, that we may really be able to serve, in our own small way, to regenerate the world . . ." [98]

To share in Mary's purity for us who do not share in her Immaculate Conception means to submit to God's purifying action within us. "Once we have put ourselves in our Lord's hands we can expect that he will handle us with vigour—always, however, to make us advance a little further within him. What price should we not be happy to pay for such an advance and such a

[94] Letter of October 15, 1915, *MM*, p. 75.
[95] Letter of December 5, 1916, *MM*, p. 149.
[96] *DM*, p. 114.
[97] Letter of December 5, 1916, *MM*, p. 149.
[98] Letter of December 8, 1918, *MM*, p. 262.

transformation." [99] The pain of growth, of failure, of loneliness, sickness and death, which we have seen form the inevitable shadow cast by universal progress, are the first objects that must be transformed by our faith into instruments of Christ's unitive power within us. "That Christ may enter deeply into us, we need alternately the work that dilates the heart and the sorrow that brings death to it, the life that enlarges a man in order that he may be sanctifiable and the death that diminishes him in order that he may be sanctified." [100]

Responding to God in Events: Communion in Suffering

The Pleroma, which is the purpose of creative union, is a communion of persons, and it is realized only by the unique and hyper-personalizing union of each individual person with God in Christ. God touches each of us immediately, acting in us triunely, the Father drawing us to the Son through the graces of attraction and influence of the Spirit within us; yet His immediate creative action within us works in harmony with and is manifested in a multitude of external events, circumstances, relationships that are continuously influencing us from without, subject to His loving providence. We can only respond to His imperceptible action within by seeing Him and cooperating actively with His creative action in those circumstances of our milieu—the divine milieu—by which He completes us and makes us one with Himself. Whether they are happy circumstances that buoy us up and develop our powers, or painful influences that tear us away from our world and ourselves, it is the same loving God who is skillfully shaping our real selves by His delicate balancing of light and shadow, for in every circumstance He is inviting us to a particular reaction, a certain decision, by which we will set the center of our existence a little more in Him. Teilhard describes this two-

[99] Letter of September 23, 1917, *MM*, p. 203.
[100] "Le Prêtre," *Ecrits*, pp. 285-302, in *HU*, p. 123.

fold action of God within us and without us, in terms of the coordinating interraction of "the two hands of God." In an intimate prayer of faith he writes:

Yes, O my God, I believe it . . . In the life which wells up in me and in the matter which sustains me, I find much more than Your gifts. It is You Yourself whom I find, You who make me participate in Your Being, You who mould me. It is through the initial control and modulation of the vital force within me, and the favourable and continuous interplay of secondary causes, that I touch, as closely as may be, the two facets of Your creative action; that I encounter, and kiss, Your two marvellous hands—the one which holds us so firmly that it is merged, in us, with the sources of life; and the other whose embrace is so wide that, at slightest pressure, all the springs of the universe respond harmoniously together.[101]

In all that happens to us, if we believe, we experience "the joy of another's action in us." [102] "Even the humiliation you feel at the thought of not making sufficient progress in the 'essential' should be for you the occasion for acts of the most sincere and intimate adoration," Teilhard counsels Marguerite. "The smaller you feel you are, the better will you adore, for you will be speaking from the inmost depths of your heart; and the better you adore, the more God will enter into your imperfections and make use of you, poor though you may be, to allow much good to radiate from you." [103] In another letter he tells her: "As to separations, we may be sure that our hearts will always bleed for them, but that is the price we must pay for our Lord's entering into us a little further." [104] When his cousin is "going through a crisis," Teilhard encourages her to seek "in close union with our Lord" a faith and "confidence in a God who is leading you triumphantly —fairer and more successful every day in his eyes—by dim and difficult paths, to his own divine center." [105]

There are some sufferings, however, that do not seem in any way capable of developing us, but rather seem bent on crushing

101 *DM*, p. 50.
102 Letter of December 28, 1916, *MM*, p. 158.
103 Letter of November 7, 1915, *MM*, pp. 79-80.
104 Letter of February 15, 1915, *MM*, p. 48.
105 Letter of September 29, 1915, *MM*, p. 70.

and destroying us: our failures, illness, ultimately death. These demand of us a much stronger faith; yet if we believe, these "seemingly meaningless and uncompensated diminishments" can become the most powerful agents of our transformation. "God, without sparing us the partial deaths, nor the final death, which form an essential part of our lives, transfigures them by integrating them in a better plan—provided we trust lovingly in Him." [106] The painful sufferings which accompany "the progressive destruction of our egoism," if we submit to God's action in them, are "very real forms of that ecstasy which is to tear us from ourselves so as to subordinate us to God," and hidden in their depths "lies a power that can dissipate egoism, bring tenderness to the heart, clarify the understanding, and reveal God." [107] In each of these partial diminishments we have an opportunity to practice, as it were, for our final surrender to God in the death which completes them, or more precisely, we progressively hand ourselves over to Him in these sufferings until the gift of ourselves culminates in the total surrender of death.

In a passage revealing the tenderness of a deep love, both for Christ and for Marguerite, Teilhard summarizes the role of diminishments, especially our own inadequacies and failure, in our progressive transformation:

Bit by bit our Lord conquers you and makes you his own . . . Entrust yourself, lose yourself blindly in your trust in our Lord, who seeks to make you worthy of himself, and will make you so, even if you are left in darkness to the end, providing you hold his hand all the time, clasping it more tightly the more you feel disappointed and saddened. Put aside every excessive concern with interior aesthetics, with your own internal state, every debilitating analysis of your precise degree of sincerity and moral integration. Right to the end we shall carry with us a burden of inconsistencies and unachieved aims: the great thing is to have found the center of unification, God, and to have tried loyally throughout our lives to make him reign in our own person—the little fragment of being that we rule and that is so little our own. When one day, which will not be long in coming (all life is brief), Jesus Christ makes himself manifest at the heart of our being, all the elements that we have worked so laboriously to orientate

[106] *DM*, p. 58.
[107] "Témoignage Fraternel," quoted in Cuénot, p. 136.

towards him will move of their own accord to group themselves in their real place.[108]

The key to our transformation through the sufferings that lead ultimately to our death is the principle of communion through diminishment which Teilhard develops in *The Divine Milieu*. Animated by the Spirit with a great longing to experience Christ in "the power of his resurrection and fellowship of his sufferings," we shall discover in the pain we suffer the loving presence of God Himself who is painfully parting the fibres of our being, as Teilhard expresses it in prayer, in order to "penetrate to the very marrow of our substance" and unite us totally in Him. The prayer continues:

The more deeply and incurably the evil is encrusted in my flesh, the more it will be You that I am harbouring—You as a loving, active principle of purification and detachment. The more the future opens before me like some dizzy abyss or dark tunnel, the more confident I may be—if I venture forward on the strength of Your word—of losing myself and surrendering myself in You, of being assimilated by Your body, Jesus.[109]

A deep and selfless, even divine, joy is known only by those "who dare to set the center of their being *outside themselves*, who dare to love Another *more than themselves*, and in some sense become this Other; which is to say, who dare to pass through death to find life." [110] And this is the joy of finding and surrendering to a Beauty greater than man, the rapture of being possessed, "which makes even the final terror" of death, "for the mystic, the climax of his bliss." [111] The death "that liberates, that breaks down the barriers that keep the soul in isolation and allows it to lose itself in God"—this is the death that Teilhard prayed would be for him a final and total communion with Christ: "to die a communion-death." [112]

[108] Letter of August 22, 1915, *MM*, p. 70.
[109] *DM*, p. 62.
[110] "La Lutte contre la Multitude," *Ecrits*, pp. 113-132, quoted in *HU*, p. 119.
[111] "Le Milieu Mystique," *Ecrits*, pp. 137-67, in *HU*, pp. 117-118.
[112] "Notes de Retraites" (unpubl.), quoted in *HU*, p. 26.

Charity:
Communion in One Body

The Christian who has found in constant prayer a faith capable of illumining his whole world; who has yielded himself progressively more and more, in each Eucharistic contact, to the unitive power of Christ's Spirit; and who has co-labored with the Spirit in generous fidelity and ever increasing purity—such a Christian has truly co-created and co-redeemed the world—his world. Each man, Teilhard explains, is a microcosm, and "though enveloped within the same universe as all other men, presents an independent center of divinization," a "partial divine milieu." God can save or unite to Himself the universe only by saving individual persons in each of whom that universe is uniquely centered. Each Christian's first task, therefore is to "make sure of his own personal sanctification—not out of egoism, but with a firm and broad understanding that the task of each one of us is to divinize the whole world in an infinitesimal and incommunicable degree." [113] *My* world, which is the same as *yours*, is yet different precisely because it is mine; and it can be united to God only *through me*. In the mystical union of co-creation, the Spirit and I unite *my* world in Jesus to the Father—we offer it to the Father's embrace. But *my* world is not the Pleroma, nor is yours; rather it is *our* world, the universe sanctified in the final communion of Christians and *their* worlds, that is in "the whole 'body of the elect,' " incorporating the universe into their common vision and love, that alone is worthy of the Father's embrace.[114] How is this final communion of individual divine milieus to be achieved? The only man whose vision and love is capable of embracing all things is Jesus, the Incarnate Word. It is Christ who "binds us and reveals us to one another." [115] To the extent that each of us begins to see and love by Christ's Spirit, to that extent we begin even now to see and love together as one, and to incorporate the world into that single vision and

[113] *DM*, pp. 122-123.
[114] *DM*, pp. 124, 126.
[115] "La Lutte contre la Multitude," *Ecrits*, pp. 113-32, in *HU*, p. 119.

unity of love that is ours who have been called to the unity of "one body and one Spirit," and who share "one hope, one Lord, one faith, one baptism." [116] At the Parousia, we shall all see God in his Pleroma as one, "through the eyes of Christ," in a vision whose brilliance and beauty will be the result of the harmonious blending of all the varied and unique "visions" of each of us. The only power capable of realizing this communion in vision, either in its beginning stages in this life or in its perfection at the Parousia is the Spirit who is drawing us into this unity primarily through our Eucharistic communion which celebrates, anticipates, and gradually creates the parousial community. As the Spirit incorporates each of us into the Risen Lord's continuous love-act of Death-Resurrection, He breaks down our self-centered isolationism and opens us to union with Christ and correlatively to union with one another. The love of the Spirit is simultaneously upward and outward, so that necessarily the more I love Christ, the more I am united with Him, the more, also, I love those whom I find in Him, who are His Body, and so the more we become one in our vision, and the more our "worlds" come together in Him who is their common Center. Thus Jesus' command to love one another expresses with divine simplicity the ultimate power of creative-union.

Christian charity, which is preached so fervently by the Gospels, is nothing else than the more or less conscious cohesion of souls engendered by their communal convergence *in Christo Jesu.* It is impossible to love Christ without loving others (in proportion as these others are moving towards Christ). And it is impossible to love others (in a spirit of broad human communion) without moving nearer to Christ. Hence automatically, by a sort of living determinism, the individual divine milieux, in proportion as they establish themselves, tend to fuse one with another; and in this association they find a boundless increase of their ardour.[117]

Teilhard is painfully aware of the struggle and suffering that alone can effect the perfection of charity. We can only unite with him in his honest confession of his "instinctive reaction to rebuff" the other man—"'the other' quite simply as 'other,' the

[116] Eph. 4:4-5.
[117] *DM*, p. 125.

one who seems to exist independently of me because his universe seems closed to mine." [118] It is this "inborn hostility" to others, this innate self-centeredness, made excessive by the example of selfishness in the world into which we were born and by our own selfish acts, that is the very core of our constant need of redemption. To love one another as Christ loves us, to see together as He sees, we must die and rise with Him daily in the Eucharist and in our lives until our final glorification in Him at our death opens us out totally to one another. In the meantime we must pray constantly: "Grant, O God, that the light of Your countenance may shine for me in the life of that 'other' . . . Grant that I may see You, even and above all, in the souls of my brothers, at their most personal, and most true, and most distant." [119] Our humble acceptance of our constant need of redemption in order to love, a need which we share with all of our brothers, with all of its various manifestations of selfishness and egoism, can become a fruitful source of an abiding compassion, which is in itself redemptive and a powerful incentive to true Christian charity. Then, in spite of our daily failures to love, our union around the Eucharist can become a genuine embodiment of our communal desire for perfect union as expressed in the conclusion of Teilhard's prayer:

Jesus, Saviour of human activity to which You have given meaning, Saviour of human suffering to which You have given living value, be also the Saviour of human unity; compel us to discard our pettiness, and to venture forth, resting upon You, into the uncharted ocean of charity.[120]

[118] DM, p. 126.
[119] DM, p. 127.
[120] DM, p. 128.

CONCLUSION

The Need for Teilhard's Spirituality Today

"Who will be the Christian to make every drop of sap from the world flow into his own movement toward the divine Trinity? It will be he who has understood that to be fully a child of God, to accomplish fully His holy will, one must show himself more diligent in earthly work than any servant of Mammon." [1] The only God who is dead in the world of today is a God who is indifferent to human progress, but this is not the Christian God. We might paraphrase our question by asking: Who will be the Christian to proclaim to the world by his life that Jesus Christ is Lord—the Lord of the Universe, who is the Center of cosmogenesis and the very Source of modern man's passion for progress —that Jesus the Saviour is, in fact, the "unknown God" [2] whose Cross is the summation and guarantee of modern man's pursuit of an ultra-humanity. Who will give clear evidence that the Incarnate God, far from despising our human efforts, has willed to *need* them, and in fact invites man to co-labor with Him in the pursuit of a goal that does not destroy but divinizes the fruits of his honest toil? Teilhard contrasts the "spirituality" of the dedicated believer today, with its characteristic virtues of compassion, eagerness to work, and a disinterestedness in the pursuit of the human task, with the somewhat distorted spirituality that the unbeliever has associated with the Christian, characterized in his

[1] "La Maîtrise du Monde et le Règne de Dieu," *Ecrits*, p. 81, quoted in Mooney, p. 150.
[2] Cf. "A Note on Progress," *FM*, p. 24.

111

eyes by a preoccupation with his own "petty salvation," a laziness disguised by a "religious" belief in the next world, and a superficial and formalistic type of charity. "The remedy, I believe," writes Teilhard, "for this slackening of the Christian effort, is always the same: to understand that God is obtained by carrying through our task as men, that Providence in no way dispenses us from effort,—that our neighbor must be loved in *himself* through love of God." [3] The remedy is, in fact, the exacting and thoroughly Christian spirituality and, ultimately, mysticism of co-creative union which Teilhard proposes in *The Divine Milieu*. The Second Vatican Council has called on all Christians to realize that their Christian vocation demands the very incarnation of their love of Christ in a faith-inspired dedication to human progress which is the essence of Teilhard's spirituality. [4]

We can only hope that Christians will respond to the Church's call to renewal by living the Gospel and Pauline spirituality in the full and integrating dimension which Teilhard uncovers, that is, in "the sort of mysticism that makes one seek passionately for God in the heart of every substance and every action." [5] This is the fullness of Christian life that "needs the sacraments, and prayer, and the apostolate, and study: all these directed to the same concrete, very precise, end" [6]—the fullness of the Body of Christ.

The world today needs, very simply, the man who in his own daily life has "transposed God . . . from the plane of the imagined (or imaginary) to the plane of the real—[for] in that lies a fortifying power and a proof of truth for all who seek to believe but for whom the world of the divine is hopelessly unreal—imaginary." [7] Teilhard, we believe, became such a man by living the mysticism of co-creative union. May we, too, show God *alive* in our world and visibly operative in Christ-Omega.

[3] Letter of July 30, 1918, *MM*, pp. 223-224.
[4] Cf. "Constitution on Church in Modern World," art. 39, 43, 57, 93 in Abbott, pp. 237, 242-43, 262, 307. The entire document is permeated with Teilhard's synthesis.
[5] Letter of March 29, 1917, *MM*, p. 190.
[6] *Ibid.*, p. 191.
[7] Quoted in Cuénot, p. 391.

Glossary of Terms

ANTHROPOGENESIS. The birth and evolution of man and his socio-political organization.

BIOGENESIS. The birth and progressive complexification of living beings, beginning at the first critical point on the axis of cosmogenesis, and continuing as the intensification of that same axis until the next critical point brought the birth of man and the beginning of noogenesis.

BIOSPHERE. The layer of non-reflective living beings which encircles the earth.

CENTER. The focal point of man's reflective consciousness and, therefore, the source and goal of noospheric (hence cosmic) convergence; Omega.

CENTRATION. The process by which the universe becomes interiorized and unified, hence spiritualized, in man.

CEREBRATION. The process observable in biological evolution by which organisms tend toward the development of more complex nervous systems and brains; noospheric cerebration is an analogous process by which man develops, through more perfect social organization and communication, a sort of collective "nervous system" and "brain."

CHRIST-OMEGA. The Risen Christ who, as the pre-existing and transcendent Source and Goal of universal becoming portrayed in Colossians and Ephesians, fulfills the demands of the Omega point postulated by the theory of a converging cosmogenesis.

CHRISTOGENESIS. The process by which the Incarnate Son assumed and suranimated with his Spirit the axis of noogenesis and continues to draw all things, in man, towards the super-synthesis of his Body.

113

CHRISTOSPHERE. The consciousness, in faith and love, of the active presence of Christ as cosmic Center or Omega, which permeates the noosphere and transforms it into the "divine milieu."

COMPLEXITY. A quality of arranged matter that is determined by the number and differentiation of elements and the degree of psychic or centrating power generating their synthesis.

COMPLEXITY-CONSCIOUSNESS. The law that appears to govern evolution. It drives matter toward ever more centered and differentiated arrangements, in which the increased psychic or centrating power pushes on to yet more differentiated and centered arrangements, a process which leads matter inevitably to spirit.

CONSCIOUSNESS. The psychic or centrating and self-determining power present in all matter from the beginning, and progressing from its most diffuse and primitive stages to its most highly focused and autonomous stage in human reflection, and continuing to progress toward the heights of co-reflection.

CONVERGENCE. The movement of evolution toward more centered and complex arrangements and ultimately toward spiritual synthesis in personal union achieved at the apex of evolution.

CO-REFLECTION. The power and act of collective self-consciousness which constitutes mankind as a unified center of communal activity.

COSMIC CHRIST. The Incarnate Son who is uniting, through his redemptive activity, the whole material universe assimilated in mankind into his own Person as his Body.

COSMOGENESIS. The birth and evolution of cosmic matter; the universe centered and in process of convergence.

CORPUSCULIZATION. The process by which matter becomes more synthesized or more arranged and centered due to the forward drive of complexity-consciousness.

CREATIVE UNION. The process by which the Triune God, by a sort of inner necessity, opposes and unites to himself the nothingness of multiplicity, drawing it to the hyper-personalizing communion and fullness of being that constitutes the Pleroma or Body of Christ.

CRITICAL POINT. A peak of complex and centered arrangement within a given sphere of possibilities, at which the axial drive of complexity-consciousness explodes into a higher sphere of complexification.

DETACHMENT. A constant drive to transcend our present state of being by seeking ever greater truth, beauty and life, and centering ourself ever more totally on the Other who is Christ.

DIAPHANY. The presence of Christ shining through the universe become transparent by faith.

DIVINIZATION. The process of perfecting and transforming man's personality through his increasingly more conscious and free union with Christ.

EVOLUTION. The process by which the universe is progressing along a permanent axis towards a final point of convergence.

GOD-OF-THE-FORWARD. God considered primarily as immanent to cosmogenesis, attained and served through detached dedication to human progress.

GOD-OF-THE-UPWARD. God considered primarily as transcendent, attained and served best by renunciation and prayer in solitude.

HOMINIZATION. The process by which mankind became progressively more reflective and its social organization became more complex.

HYPER-, SUPER-, SUPRA-. Indicating a dimension attainable only in and through the divinely free operation of Christ.

IMMANENT. Within and organically united with the historical unfolding of cosmic evolution.

IN-COILING. The tendency of reflective beings to converge inwardly upon themselves in a process of increasing interiorization and autonomy.

INTERIORIZATION. The process of in-coiling by which mankind becomes increasingly more self-conscious and autonomous, and by which the material universe in mankind becomes spiritual and personal.

IRREVERSIBILITY. The necessity inherent in a converging cosmogenesis become reflective, to continue its evolution toward the highest possible co-reflective synthesis in union with a pre-existent and transcendent Center of convergence; immortality.

NEO-ANTHROPOCENTRICISM. A man-centered view of the universe, based not on the ancient misconception of man's spacial relation to the rest of the universe, but on his capacity and responsibility to direct the course of evolution toward its term of convergence.

NOODYNAMIC. Capable of generating the psychic energy necessary for man to continue his efforts to progress in noogenesis, especially by stimulating his hope.

NOOGENESIS. The birth and evolution of reflective consciousness toward the highest possible co-reflective synthesis achieved in personal union.

NOOSPHERE. The layer of reflective beings who are encircling the earth with an increasingly complex and unifying network of communications and collective thought.

OMEGA. 1) The apex of converging cosmogenesis; the center of ultimate synthesis in the noosphere and the term of noogenesis, and hence cosmogenesis; 2) The pre-existent and transcendent superperson, loving and lovable and omnipresent as the activating Center, Source and Goal of noogenesis, a description fulfilled by the risen Christ portrayed in John and Paul.

OMEGALIZATION. The process of heightening man's consciousness of Christ-Omega, and of drawing him, and in him the whole universe, into the differentiated union with Christ-Omega which constitutes the Pleroma; Pleromization; Creative Union.

PERSONALIZATION. The effect of noogenesis, and more perfectly, of Christogenesis, by which the universe becomes personal by being assimilated into the co-reflective synthesis of mankind united; ultra- or hyper-personalization is that achieved by union with God in Christ; pleromization or creative union aims at a supra-personalizing union which, correspondingly, supra-individuates and perfects each personality.

PLANETIZATION. The process by which the diverse races and civilizations tend to synthesize and converge in a single planetary civilization, sharing a rich and unified co-reflective vision of reality.

PLEROMA. The fullness of all being, in which the created many are drawn into the union and inter-personal relations of the divine Persons through their identity with the Incarnate Son as his Body.

PLEROMIZATION. The process by which the Pleroma is achieved through the creative-redemptive activity of the divine Persons and the collaboration of mankind; the process of creative and co-creative union.

RADIAL ENERGY. The axial drive of evolution which moves the process of cosmogenesis toward ever more complex, centered arrangements, and ever more interiorized spiritual syntheses.

REFLECTION. The power and act of self-consciousness which constitutes man as a centered and autonomous person and the director of cosmogenesis.

SOCIAL EUGENICS. A science of the future which will aim at perfecting the organization of the world civilization.

SPIRIT OF THE EARTH. The compassionate concern to unite in the common task of mankind to build the Earth, that is, to build the single planetary civilization which will form the basis of mankind's final union.

SURANIMATE (or SUPERANIMATE). Transfuse with greater power, as the Risen Christ super-charges the forward thrust of evolution, or radial energy, with the power of the Spirit.

SUPERNATURAL. Pertaining to the totally gratuitous end and process of creative union or pleromization.

SYNTHESIS. The process of organizing all the elements of the Universe, according to their actual interrelatedness, into a single unified vision of reality, ultimately in the Pleroma.

TANGENTIAL ENERGY. The attracting force within beings which draws those of like complexity together at each successive stage of complexification in preparation for the next higher stage.

TOTALIZATION. The progressive unification of all personal energy, individual and communal, in a self-giving love of Christ-Omega.

TRANSCENDENT. Superior to and independent of the historical unfolding of cosmogenesis, and not requiring it *absolutely* for existence.

TRINITIZATION. The process of inter-personal relations in which the divine Persons oppose and unite themselves to one another, and which in some sense necessitates an extension of itself outside the intimacy of these relations, in the process of creative union or pleromization.

ULTRA-HUMANITY. The final state of mankind at the completion of the Pleroma, when man, individually and collectively, will have attained a super-personalization and super-union within the Trinity.

Bibliography

I. Works by Pierre Teilhard de Chardin

Books by Teilhard de Chardin and Anthologies of His Writings

Oeuvres de Pierre Teilhard de Chardin:

I. *Le phénomène humain,* Paris, 1955. American edition: *The Phenomenon of Man,* tr. B. Wall, revised translation, New York: Harper Torchbooks, 1965.

II. *L'apparition de l'homme,* Paris, 1956. American edition: *The Appearance of Man,* tr. J. Cohen, New York: Harper & Row, 1965.

III. *La vision du passe,* Paris, 1957. American edition: *The Vision of the Past,* New York: Harper & Row, 1967.

IV. *Le milieu divin,* Paris, 1957. American edition: *The Divine Milieu,* tr. B. Wall, A. Dru, N. Lindsay, D. MacKinnon, *et al.,* New York: Harper & Brothers, 1960.

V. *L'avenir de l'homme,* Paris, 1959. American edition: *The Future of Man,* tr. N. Denny, New York, Harper & Row, 1964.

VI. *L'énergie humaine,* Paris, 1962.

VII. *L'activation de l'énergie,* Paris, 1963.

VIII. *Le groupe zoologique humaine,* Paris, 1965. American edition: *Man's Place in Nature,* New York: Harper & Row, 1966.

IX. *Science et Christ,* Paris, 1965.

Ecrits du temps de la guerre (1916-1919), Paris, 1965.

Hymne de l'univers, Paris, 1961. American edition: *Hymn of the Universe,* tr. S. Bartholomew, New York: Harper & Row, 1965.

Construire la Terre, Paris, 1958, Cahier I. (This is a combination of excerpts from the following works:

1. Ch. I. Extracts from "Sauvons l'humanité," *Science et Christ, Oeuvres de Pierre Teilhard de Chardin,* IX (Paris: editions du Seuil, 1965), pp. 167-191.

119

2. Ch. II. Extracts from "L'esprit de la terre," *L'énergie humaine, Oeuvres,* VI, pp. 23-57.
3. Ch. III. Extracts from "L'énergie humaine," *Oeuvres,* VI, pp. 141-200.
4. Ch. IV. Extracts from "Réflexions sur le progrès," *L'activation de l'énergie, Oeuvres,* V, pp. 27-63. ("Reflections on Progress," *The Future of Man,* pp. 61-81.)
5. Ch. V. "Sur les bases possibles d'un credo commun," written by Teilhard on a questionnaire sent out by UNESCO, published here in its entirety.

Blondel et Teilhard de Chardin, Paris, 1965. American edition: *Pierre Teilhard de Chardin, Maurice Blondel: Correspondence,* New York: Herder & Herder, 1967.

Other Published Essays of Teilhard de Chardin

"La parole attendue," *Cahiers Pierre Teilhard de Chardin. 4. La parole attendue,* Paris, 1963, pp. 22-29.
"La pensée du Père Teilhard de Chardin," *Les études philosophiques,* 10 (1955), 580-581.

Essays of Teilhard de Chardin
Unpublished as of April, 1966

"La route de l'ouest," 1932.
"Christologie et évolution," 1933.
"Comment je crois," 1934.
"Le Christ évoluteur," 1942.
"Introduction à la vie chrétienne," 1944.
"Christianisme et évolution," 1945.
"Comment je vois," 1948.
"Le coeur de la matière," 1950.
"Ce que le monde attend en ce moment de l'Eglise de Dieu: une généralisation et un approfondissement du sens de la croix," 1952.
"Contingence de l'univers et goût humain de survivre," 1953.
"Le Christique," 1955.

II. SECONDARY SOURCES

Braybrooke, Neville (ed.). *Teilhard de Chardin, Pilgrim of the Future.* New York: Seasbury, 1964.

Cuénot, Claude. *Teilhard de Chardin*. Baltimore: Helicon, 1965.

de Lubac, Henri. *The Religion of Teilhard de Chardin*. New York: Desclee, 1967.

———. *Teilhard de Chardin, The Man and His Meaning*. New York: Hawthorn, 1965.

Faricy, Robert, S.J. *Teilhard de Chardin's Theology of the Christian in the World*. New York: Sheed and Ward, 1967.

Mooney, Christopher, S.J. *Teilhard de Chardin and the Mystery of Christ*. New York: Harper and Row, 1965.

III. Related Works

Abbott, Walter, S.J. *The Document of Vatican II*. New York: America Press, 1966.

Boros, Ladislaus, S.J. *The Mystery of Death*. New York: Herder, 1965.

The Canisianum Editors. *The Christian and the World*. New York: P. J. Kenedy, 1965.

———. *The Church*. New York: P. J. Kenedy, 1963.

Cerfaux, Lucien. *Christ in the Theology of St. Paul*. New York: Herder, 1959.

Durwell, F. X., C.SS.R. *The Resurrection*. New York: Sheed and Ward, 1960.

Maritain, Jacques. *Creative Intuition in Art and Poetry*. New York: Pantheon Books, 1955.

Moroux, Jean. *The Mystery of Time*. New York: Desclee, 1962.

Rahner, Karl, S.J. *The Christian Commitment*. New York: Sheed and Ward, 1963.

———. *Nature and Grace*. New York: Sheed and Ward, 1964.

———. *On the Theology of Death*. New York: Herder, 1961.

Schoonenberg, P., S.J. *God's World in the Making*. Pittsburgh: Duquesne University Press, 1964.

———. *Man and Sin*. Notre Dame, Ind.: University of Notre Dame Press, 1965.

van Caster, Marcel, S.J. "Human and Christian Meaning of Work," a reprint from *Lumen Vitae*, 20 (1965), No. 2.

Key to Abbreviations of Teilhard's Works used in notes:

AM:	*The Appearance of Man*
CT:	*Construire la Terre*
Correspondence:	*Pierre Teilhard de Chardin, Maurice Blondel: Correspondence*

DM:	*The Divine Milieu*
Ecrits:	*Ecrits du temps de la guerre*
FM:	*The Future of Man*
HU:	*Hymn of the Universe*
MPN:	*Man's Place in Nature*
Oeuvres:	*Oeuvres de Pierre Teilhard de Chardin*
PM:	*The Phenomenon of Man*
MM:	*The Making of a Mind*

DATE DUE